Convicted:
One Hundred Days

Devotions to Help Physically and
Spiritually Incarcerated People

CHAPLAIN PAUL

ISBN 978-1-63961-406-6 (paperback)
ISBN 978-1-63961-407-3 (digital)

Christian Faith Publishing, Inc.
832 Park Avenue
Meadville, PA 16335
www.christianfaithpublishing.com

All scripture references are from the English Standard Version unless otherwise noted.

Printed in the United States of America

These devotionals started as Bible study papers I wrote and sent to inmates in my prison during the COVID shutdown. The target audience was male inmates, but I hope the words can still have some value in teaching and encouragement to others as well. God has blessed and given me a platform of ministry as a prison chaplain, and I thank Good News Jail and Prison Ministry for their important role in that. I also want to thank my wife for encouraging me to write and put these thoughts in a book. I want to thank Brandon for his words, which led me to come up with the title. I thank the inmates and COs of YCP who gave encouraging feedback on these devotionals. I trust God will use this book to challenge and encourage you wherever you are in life right now.

Introduction

What Will You Do With Jesus?

This is the world's biggest question. Everyone has to answer it including you. You might say, "I don't want to answer that question" or "I will answer that later," but those responses are the same as "I don't want anything to do with Jesus. I would rather think about other stuff." Okay, and that is your choice, but be clear that you are rejecting Him. A "No, for now," is still a no. But you are reading this book, so the question may have gotten your attention, and maybe you already have decided to acknowledge Jesus in some way in your life. It appears you do not want to reject Him fully, so that brings us back to what will you actually do with Jesus. Let's look at a few possible answers:

1. Use Jesus

Maybe you are not sure what to do with Jesus, but you do not want to ignore Him because what if life became bad without Him? "Maybe, as long as I go to church or pray every once in a while, I will be blessed, and God will give me stuff—or at least not make my life miserable." What are you doing with Jesus? You are basically using Him as a good luck charm. "I have tried a bunch of other things in life, let's try Jesus and see if He makes things work out for me." This is not a healthy relationship. Do not think that you can use Jesus.

2. Play the game

Maybe you just play the game with Jesus. You know the game, right? If your mom asks if you are reading the Bible, you say yes whether you do or not. You only use good, clean words in front of the chaplain. You even go to church on Christmas and Easter. Twice a year church is good enough, right? What you are doing is playing a game. The game is to have the minimum amount of Jesus possible to appease your conscience and keep you from feeling guilty. I mean, deep down you know you should really be following Jesus more, but then you would have to change too much because you know Jesus wouldn't be happy with a few things in your life. So you have just enough Jesus that you can feel, like you are better than the other guy. And if you are better than someone else, well, how mad could God get at you?

3.   Follow Jesus…in here

Okay, maybe you truly are sincere about following Jesus. Maybe you really do accept Him fully and want to live like Him. And you do. Or at least as long as you are in here. But when you get out, that is a different story. Okay, let's talk. What is the problem? Obviously, a part of you knows that Jesus truly is the answer. Great. In here, everything is pretty regulated, and you find it easy to follow Jesus. But out there…well, too many temptations. So at least we are partway there. But you are going to need to make some really hard decisions and do some really hard things to get to the next level. Of course, even though it is difficult, you need to follow through and do these hard things because the next level below is the right answer.

4.   Jesus is Lord of your life

This is where you decide to accept the gift of God, which is life through Jesus and what He did for us. You realize He is the only way (**John 14:6**). You realize Jesus's way is the only way to live. You decide to live out your life like Jesus would. You do not always succeed, but you are trying and moving in His direction every day. Some days you have to make some really hard decisions to leave the path of sin—that is hard, especially when other people do not put Jesus that high in their lives. But you know it is worth it. You know God is the only one to truly follow, and He showed us the way through Jesus. This sounds pretty radical. It is. And it only is because a lot of people don't want to change their lives that much. We want our cake and eat it too—we want Jesus, but we want a bit of the sinful world too. Nope. Can't do it. Either Jesus is Lord of your life or He is not. God is full of grace to us, but you will not enjoy the full blessings of God in your life without being all-in. Do not be afraid of a full life change to Him.

Look, it is a radical decision to truly make Jesus Lord of your life. But something is always ruling you—maybe it is that woman, or maybe that drug or alcohol. Maybe it is those other guys you are trying to be like or get approval from. Maybe it is just your own sinful desires. But it is only when Jesus is fully ruling over us that life can change for the better. The question is will you let Him change you?

I hope these devotionals will be encouraging to you because God loves you. I hope these devotionals will be challenging to you because God wants you to progress closer to Him. Keep Him first every day. What will you do with Jesus?

Day 1   Abraham's Faith   Genesis 12

Abraham is pretty famous in the Bible for a few reasons, and we will look at one of those today. He was living way back in an era before technology and was asked by God to move. Read **Genesis 12:1–4**. It seems pretty straightforward—God asked Abraham to leave his country and his "father's house" to go to a new place, but we need to see this through the eyes of that era. There was no GPS for Abraham to use. He could not go online and look at pictures of the new place. He had no realtor to help him choose a house. He also was leaving his relatives without the ability to Facetime or text them. He was going to change his whole life to go into the unknown because God told him to. That is faith.

Now look at **Hebrews 11:8–10 and 13–16**. These are powerful verses describing Abraham's faith. He trusted that God would take care of him, so he left the comfort of his homeland for the new place. But it wasn't really about the new land. In verses 10 and 16, it says that Abraham was looking forward to a permanent home—heaven. He was not concerned about the details here on earth because he knew God is in control and that this life is only temporary. The benefits of trusting God far outweigh what the world can offer us. Verse 15 shows us that if they focused on what this world has to offer and if they wanted the easy path, they could have returned to where things were comfortable, but they did not do this. They understood that this world is not the end. Eternity is the end, so why wouldn't we listen to the One who has eternity in His hand? This is the root of Abraham's faith. He acknowledged God, listened to God, and was willing to change how and where he lived because he trusted in God.

Nice stuff, right? How do you think it applies to you? Think about it a minute. I will wait.

God wants you to move forward. God wants you to go to a new life. Why is change so hard? Why don't we like change? It is unknown, right? We have that fear of the unknown. If our current situation is bad, we worry that change could be worse because at least we know how to live and make it in our current bad situation. The bad known is better than the questionable unknown. Or so we think.

You see, God is calling all of us to a new way of life—it is like He is calling us to a new country, like Abraham. But we are often afraid of change—change is hard! Yet we have to understand that we can never get to a better place without change. (Say it slowly now.) "We can never get to a better place without change." We have to move. Abraham learned this, and the key to his moving was that he trusted the One who told him to move. We have to trust that God knows what he is doing. When God says to trust Him and put Him first, He means that He will be with us in special ways and will guide our life. We have to trust that and act on that.

So do you trust God? For real, for real. If you are not sure, then you need to get to know Him better. You need to see who Jesus is in Matthew, Mark, Luke, and John in the Bible, and you need to understand how God has got you—read Philippians, Colossians, and Hebrews in the Bible. You need to know God well enough that you will trust Him, no matter what. That is a big statement but is true.

Once you trust God, you need to get specific with what you need to change. The funny thing is that we usually know exactly what we need to change. We know we have some friends we need to get rid of—but we don't because we don't trust that God can replace those friends, and we fear we will be alone. See how this starts with faith so we can do what we know God wants us to do? What else do you need to change? Some change is getting rid of things in our lives while other change is adding to our lives—making church a bigger part of our week in the future, making time with God bigger right now. I know I always need to change how I react to and spend time with people. I always need to be more compassionate to the needs of others and be willing to reach out and serve others more. What about you?

Look, the whole point of this lesson is that every one of us needs to change, and we are slow to do that because of fear, but we MUST have faith over fear, like Abraham. He did take a step of faith that was scary for him at that time, but his life wound up being better because God will always go with us when we step out by faith. Think about, plan, and start taking that next step in your faith walk with God. He *will* be with you every step of the way.

Day 2   Remember God

Are you forgetful? I usually have to write things down to remember them. Jesus worked with people who forgot things—just like us. Sometimes they forgot who Jesus is. Can you imagine forgetting that? I feel like if we were with Jesus, we would never forget anything He did, but His disciples forgot a pretty big lesson about who Jesus is. Start by reading **Mark 6:30–44**. Then read **Mark 8:1–9**. These are pretty famous passages. What stands out to you from them? Before moving on, I am interested that in both passages, Jesus was filled with compassion for the people. In the first one, He realized they were as sheep having no shepherd—they had no purpose to life. So Jesus taught them (more on that in a few days). In the second passage, the people listened to Him teach so much, they ran out of food, and Jesus had compassion on their bellies! In both, Jesus really cared about the people hearing God's word. Interesting.

Now read our main section, **Mark 8:14–21**. In the passage, by the way, Jesus says in verse 15 to watch out for the leaven of the false teachers—that leaven is literally yeast, but God often used it as a metaphor for false teaching. Jesus was warning the disciples not to mix Jesus's truth with others' false teaching. BUT the disciples missed the point because they were focused on something else. Someone forgot the food! And they were in a boat, so they couldn't get more than the one loaf of bread they had! Have you ever gone somewhere and forgotten food or forgotten a water bottle? Little kids usually forget their water bottles at home, and then when they remember to bring the bottle, they leave it out somewhere and forget to bring it home. Half of the job of being a parent is running around finding and picking up your kids' stuff!

Back to the disciples. In chapter 8, verse 16, all they can talk about is their lack of food, even though Jesus was trying to teach them something more important (verse 15). We see Jesus actually get upset with them here. Notice as He scolds them, He says in verse 18, "Do you not remember?" So Jesus reminds them of the two feedings and how much food was left over—what a miracle! And yet the disciples were pretty concerned that they were going to get hungry. Hmmm. What were they missing? They were forgetting who was in the boat with them! It was Jesus! We are not really told the conclusion of this conversation or if the disciples figured it out—but we know if they had any needs, Jesus would take care of them. They did not need to worry about their lack of food and could focus on Jesus's important teaching. Remember what He has done already!

All right. What is the big idea here? Was there ever a time in your life when you felt God was really close to you, and you were seeing Him guide your life? I hope so. Do you remember that time each day now? Probably not. See, we are just as forgetful as the disciples. Some days we feel really close to God, and others we feel distant and forget who He is. Remember, Jesus is the same—He is still near you and wants to help you. He cares for you—do not forget that. Ever. If He has done something for you in the past, write it down on paper or on your heart. Remember it. If He shows you a special verse in the Bible, write it down and memorize it. Usually, what happens is we forget those times as the weeks go by—the newness of God's hand on our heart goes away, and we forget who Jesus is, just like the disciples. We only look at what we need right now (or think we need) and worry and panic, forgetting that Jesus can guide and provide. Never forget things He has done for you.

If you are new in a relationship with God and don't have a long history with Him in your life, you still have something huge to never forget—that He has saved you from your sins—that He loves you that much (**John 3:16**). Never forget who He is. He has got you because He saved you. If you are not new to this Jesus relationship, you also need to never forget that the One who can provide for you is in the boat with you (like He was with the disciples). One of the keys of growing closer to God is a daily remembering (prayer, thinking, meditating) of how He is with me, how He loves me, and how He died to save me. Take time to remember Him each day. Trust Him to take care of you today and tomorrow. Don't forget God.

Day 3   Jesus (Part 1)   Luke 2

The main character of the Bible is Jesus. Over the coming days, we will focus on Jesus and some of the things He did and taught. Each time, we will try to have a lesson for our lives now, while trying to understand more and more who Jesus is and what that should mean in our lives going forward. Today, we will start at the beginning; let's see when Jesus came to earth. It is a familiar story that is especially shared in Luke 2. Let's see what happened and then remember one big important lesson for us.

Do you have a child? Were you there for his/her birth? That is a big, emotional question, right? A newborn baby coming into the world is quite a big deal. Parents just want the baby and mother to be healthy. After that, we worry about the world our little one is growing up in. **Luke 2:1–20** shares about when Jesus was born into the world. Politically, Rome was in charge and required everyone to register in their original family hometown, so Joseph and Mary had to go to Bethlehem, which was too small a place to handle the crush of visitors. This led them to have to stay in a barn since the inn was full. From this incident, we learn Jesus's first bed was a manger—sounds sweet, but a manger was actually used to feed animals. In this passage, we also see the shepherds, who were told about Jesus's arrival by the angels, since it was important that someone besides Mary and Joseph be told this was the Christ that was born, the One who was going to save His people from their sins. Jesus is God come to human flesh—so that we could understand God and His love for us. This is why Jesus went to the cross—to pay for our sins so we could go to God. This is true love. Read **John 1:14** carefully. Jesus was how we were able to see the glory of God in a way that we could clearly understand. He came full of God's truth (that we people are sinners and in trouble with God) and full of God's grace (that God loves us so much, He wants to enable us to be right with him).

Now, I want to look at the shepherds especially. They must have been pretty special people to receive the word right from angels. But that is the thing—they were not special at all. Who were shepherds? At this time in history, they would be the uneducated men who had low skills, so they were put with sheep. This is not like today where farmers have large plots of land and great understanding of how to do their job. No, this was the Roman Empire time where the best of people would join the army or be able to do business under the Roman system. So shepherds were pretty simple people. They did not have the opportunities that many other people had. They spent their time with animals and just needed to lead those sheep to fields of grass and make sure none of the sheep ran away. It was a low job in a time when people were biased toward the wealthy. Favoritism ran through society, but the shepherds would be no one's favorite (they smelled like sheep, after all).

Jesus was the God of the universe, the Creator (**John 1:1–4**). He deserved to come to earth and be born in a palace, but He wasn't. He was literally born in a barn. Now, if you saw a castle on a mountaintop, do you think you could walk right up to it and walk in? How about a rich mansion—just ring the doorbell and take a tour? Of course not. Usually, those places are gated so that common people don't bother them. Now, what about an old barn? We could totally stop and walk into an old barn and be welcome to see it and visit. The barn is a simple place and is pretty welcoming to all.

Here is the point. If Jesus was born in a palace, it would be clear He would only be coming for the rich and famous. Jesus was born in a barn. His first guests? Shepherds. It is clear that Jesus came for everybody. Jesus wanted no human barriers for anyone coming to Him from the very start. The shepherds were allowed to visit and then became the first missionaries by telling everyone in town about Jesus (**Luke 2:20**). This is so beautiful and reminds us we are always welcome to come to Jesus. He truly wants to help real people. It does not matter who you are—Jesus wants you; stay close to Him. This also means Jesus wants the guy next to you. We might not care about some people in the pod—just remember that God does. He cares about everyone you are with right now. We need to not differentiate between people but represent Jesus to everyone. God wants an open door between people and Him. That is why shepherds were chosen to visit Jesus first. What great news for us and for those around us. Jesus came for us! May this thought bring us a little bit (or a lot) of joy each day.

As we go through this series, we will look at what Jesus did and what He taught. Today, a bit of His teaching. To be honest, most of what He taught is hard to actually follow. His teaching really challenges us. Today, we will read only two verses, **Luke 6:37–38**. What do you think Jesus is saying here? Why is this important for us to follow? How can we follow this? And think about how the world would be a better place if we followed these verses, but why is it so hard to actually do?

Okay, these verses are basically telling us three things: don't judge other people, forgive, and give generously. To be honest, all three of these things are hard to do. Let's start with judging. We judge others all the time. We can always find people we think are worse than us; we shake our head at the stories we hear about that person or even what we see that person do (#smh). The problem—when I am judging others in my head, I am not thinking about my issues and what I need to do to get closer to God. I know in my life I can get distracted from growing in Jesus when I think about others and shake my head at them. I start thinking better about myself than I should because I am comparing myself to that guy instead of comparing myself to God. He is my only standard and goal. Jesus commented on this idea in **Matthew 7:3–5**. We are so concerned about someone else we forget our own issues that we should be focusing on. Why do we do this? Read **Proverbs 26:22**. We like it. We like hearing whispers about other people. This is why there are so many gossip magazines and trashy TV shows looking into people's lives. We like it, and we feel good about ourselves since we are not those people. Jesus says that it is not our job to judge everyone else, so stop. We should be looking at ourselves and judging how close we are getting to acting like Jesus!

Then Jesus says to forgive. We have been forgiven so much by God—so now we need to forgive others. Jesus told a parable about this concept in **Matthew 18:21–35**. This is a good parable to read because it reminds us how God has forgiven us of so much more than what others have done to us. Reread that last sentence. It is actually a hard statement to write because I know that some of you have been hurt a lot in this life. Your pain is real. While that is true, we must come back to how we have not lived in the glory of our Creator God. We have often chosen our own way and failed because of it—yet we have forgiveness in Christ. How about that? God forgives me. Let that thought sink in but then remember to forgive others. Revenge leads us nowhere, while forgiveness allows a new start for the offender and the forgiver.

Thirdly, Jesus says to give in verse 38. He actually says that we should give because God sees us and will use the same measuring cup to give back to us. This is a metaphor that Jesus wants us to understand. If we are using a small cup to give to others (not giving much and not caring for others much), then God will use that same small cup to give to us. The point is that it benefits everyone if we are generous. But wait, does that mean that if we give money, we will be given more money? No, it does not say that here. It just says that God will give to us—we might be given peace and comfort—which is actually more valuable than money, even though we don't always see it that way. The point is to care for others and do not obsess about money. Don't be the man Jesus told about in His parable found in **Luke 12:13–21**. The rich man in that story lived for earthly riches and forgot what was most important in life. This is a reason to be generous—so we don't become too focused on money. Be generous with your time also. There are hurting people around you that might need a friend and definitely need Jesus. Give of yourself and your time to others so they can see Jesus through you. That is the best kind of giving.

Jesus is teaching a radical new way of living in these verses. Rather than living for self, it is all about God and others. This is hard. Can we truly care for others? We will only do that when we stop judging them, start forgiving others, and give to them (our time and friendship). The world gives us messages that tell us we deserve ours, so we better look out for ourselves. God says, "I've got you so you can go help and give to others." Jesus lived this out for real. May we follow in His path.

Day 5   Jesus (Part 3)   Luke 12:32–34
(and Ecclesiastes)

Today, in just a few short verses, Jesus gets at the biggest question we can ask about ourselves: What am I living for? What is my purpose for living? Read **Luke 12:32–34**. What stands out to you from these verses?

1. Verse 32 starts with an important truth for us to believe. God wants what is best for us. It says that God the Father wants to give us the kingdom. That means life with God. It is the promise of eternal life as well as a joyous life now on earth. It is based in living according to Jesus's teaching— that is how we get to the joyous life now. Last lesson we saw Jesus emphasize giving and forgiveness—this is how we live in God's kingdom now—by being free from anger and conflict through forgiveness, since we have been forgiven by God. Too often, we think we know what is best for us, and we chase life through parties, "good times," and hanging out with people who are not good for us. Jesus says that God wants us to enjoy living according to His kingdom— God's kingdom is a totally different mindset from living for this world. God knows living for Him is best for us—the problem is that *we* do not always remember that fact.

2. Jesus describes living for God's kingdom in verses 33–34. The first thing He mentions is giving instead of getting. This will bring us true joy, but we don't naturally believe that. We live life trying to fill our money bags rather than emptying them to help others. Now, you understand here that Jesus is talking about a mindset, not just money. If my life goal is to live for this world's pleasures, I will live my life in a very selfish way. I will be concerned about how I can get ahead (because other people don't really matter) and how I can have a good time. A lot of people just live for the week-

end. They live for the party. After years of living that way, what is left? Read **Ecclesiastes 5:10–17** and **Ecclesiastes 4:1–11**. The author tried to live for money and pleasure, but in the end, he saw that it was all worthless. Have you just been living for this world's pleasure? What kind of life do you see that being ten years from now? Jesus knows this kind of living is empty. He wants better for us.

3. Jesus says to live for heaven—to live for God's kingdom, which will truly last. This is a life that gives and forgives. This is a life that tries to be a peacemaker and helper, one that loves God and loves others. It starts with understanding and remembering how God loves us so much that Jesus came to die for our sins. We get what we don't deserve because of Him (**John 3:16**). When we understand that, we can live a life that truly cares for others and loves others. Look also at **Ecclesiastes 12:13–14**. It is the same conclusion that living for God is the only way to live. Now, in Luke 12:34, there is a warning to guard your heart. Be careful—the world sucks us in and makes us care about things that do not matter. People fight and argue and hurt others so they can get ahead or get a dollar, which gets wasted anyway. Our heart needs to be focused on God alone.

4. Let me conclude by emphasizing giving one more time. Jesus says in verse 33 to sell and give to the needy. He is showing a general lifestyle of giving—of caring for others more than myself. You might say that you don't have money, but you can still give of yourself, your energy, and your time. Give to others. I like **Ecclesiastes 11:1–2**. The idea in verse 1 is that you throw your bread out there—it is your time and energy. You give that to others. And then after many days, it will come back to you—people will also care for you. Giving and living selflessly is contagious and can spread among those you are with. In verse 2, it challenges us to give to seven people. Wait, even eight people. It helps others in their time of need ("disaster"). The main point is not about the number seven or eight. The idea is

to give and then give some more. Don't say, I gave today and that is enough—that is when that eighth person comes along who needs help. Give of yourself, your time, and energy to others so they, too, can know Jesus and have true purpose for living. Jesus in Luke wants us to understand that our heart can get easily distracted by this life. Keep it close to God. He is what matters, and we can show that through our love for God and other people. What are you living for? Jesus came to give us eternal life and to give us meaning in life until we get to heaven. Look to Him and be strong in Him today.

Let's look at more of the teachings of Jesus! Today, read **Matthew 9:35–38**. What is Jesus truly teaching here? What do you think this means for you?

These verses are pretty famous and important in the Bible. Jesus is healing and teaching, He understands the people are wandering through life without much direction ("sheep without a shepherd"), and He asks His disciples to pray for more workers to tell them the purpose of life (which is Jesus, by the way—He is our purpose for life). Jesus uses a metaphor of a ripe farmer's field that is ready to be harvested but needs someone to go out and pick all the crops. The idea is that there are lots of people who are lost in life—lots! Now, they just need people to tell them about Jesus, but sadly there is a shortage of people sharing about Jesus. So here are a few things we can learn from these verses.

1. Jesus cared about people's physical needs. Jesus saw that these people needed good health, and He could do something about that. Jesus cares about people's needs, and so should we. In the famous parable of the Good Samaritan (**Luke 10:25–37**), Jesus taught that the true follower of God did not just say the right words but actually cared about another person enough to help. As followers of Jesus, we should be caring for others' physical needs and helping them out.

2. Jesus cared about people's spiritual needs. Notice that while Jesus was healing, He became burdened because these people were like lost sheep. They had no real purpose in living but were wandering aimlessly like sheep. If we do not have Jesus—if we do not have hope for the life after this life, then what do we have? People in this world are chasing a lot of things to find meaning in life. Some just seek money and pleasure. Some just try to have some peace. Some try

to be the boss over everyone else and seek power. Some try to help others or save the planet (a little more noble, but without Christ, it is only temporary help). These are all reasons to live, but they are all based in this life only. Life is short, and then there is eternity. Are we ready to meet our Creator? That is why Jesus came. He made the way for us to get to a holy God who loves us. God is just looking for us to acknowledge Him and see Him for who He is (**James 4:10, 1 Peter 5:6**). He wants to give people true hope for this life AND eternity (**John 10:10**). Jesus is truly sad here about the people He is helping, since they do not know what they are doing with life. Jesus cares about our spiritual needs.

3. The fields are ripe. This means the amount of people in the world who are lost is great. Most people in the world are in need of hearing about Jesus. Most of the people we interact with each day need Jesus. He was saying this verse standing among a crowd of people—He saw that so many of them needed hope and truth for their life.

4. The workers are few. Ahh, here is the issue. How many people are actually sharing about Jesus to the world? Jesus says the workers are few, especially compared to the needs of people in the world. I think this means we should be praying for more people to come to Jesus AND be praying for followers of Jesus to be bold about Jesus. This is a major problem. Many who follow Jesus are pretty quiet about it. Many who follow Jesus still fear social isolation, so we don't say anything. Jesus says do not fear; His Spirit will be with us (**1 Peter 4:12–14**). Some believers have the opposite problem and just yell at others. The Bible says we need to be ready to tell others about Jesus with "gentleness and respect" (**1 Peter 3:15**). Some might say, "I don't have all the answers to tell others," but if you know Jesus, you can certainly point them to Jesus, who does have all the answers. We are all on this journey through life together, so

it is okay to not have every answer right now—but let us all look to the One who does have answers.

Do not fear. Care about others. Offer them hope. If they don't want it, that is between them and God, but give people a chance to hear about the One who can change their lives. Let them see your life changed. Your changed life is an amazing testimony of God's power. Helping others come to Jesus and have true hope in their lives is one of the greatest things we can do with our lives. The harvest is ready, but workers are few. Be a worker for Jesus.

Day 7   Jesus (Part 5)   Matthew 15:10–20

I trust that God is guiding your steps. Each day renew your strength and hope in Him. He will remain with you wherever you are. Today, we will look at **Matthew 15:10–20**. Take a few minutes to read it and think about what Jesus is saying here. How might this teaching apply to your life?

Jesus calls the people and tells them an important truth in verse 11: It is not what goes in our mouth that hurts us but what comes out. Then there is a little controversy about that statement before Jesus explains it in more detail in verses 17–20. Why was this controversial in its time? What does it mean for us today? Let's take a look.

1. God doesn't want "religious" activity. He explains in verse 17 that there is nothing spiritual about food. In verse 20, he says washing your hands does not get you closer to God. These were the religious acts of the day—the Pharisees (verse 12) did these acts to show how close to God they were. This is why they are blind. They thought they could impress God by not eating certain food or by washing their hands. It is not that these are bad things to do—it is just that they are all about me. Look what I can do. I can wash! I can go without eating those foods. Today, many religious people also have religious activities that make them feel good about themselves but actually benefit no one. Maybe we think we get points if we attend church and wear certain clothes there—nothing wrong with going to church (we should), but to do it so we get points with God? No! But a lot of people do this—that is why churches are really packed with people on Christmas and Easter—lots of people trying to get points with God.

2. God loves a heart that is not proud or selfish. Look at the list in verse 19. God is not happy with these things which are found in our hearts. You understand that all the sinful

acts in verse 19 start with a heart that is sinful and far from God. This is why Jesus says that evil comes out of our heart rather than into our body through eating (verse 10). Before there is a murder, there is hatred in our hearts for someone else. Before there is adultery, there is selfishness (I want to sleep with someone else today, so I will). Before there is theft, there is selfishness (I don't care about your property. I want it). Before there is slander, there is selfishness and revenge (I will talk bad about you, so I look good. Besides, you said stuff about me, so it is on). These are the attitudes God says to avoid so that we can avoid the sins which follow. All these sins start in our heart and keep us from being close to God.

3. Guard your heart. Isn't this Jesus's point? Sin is not eating the wrong food—it is harboring hate, which turns into something else. It is giving in to my desires and lusts regardless of who is hurt in the process. It is selfishness rather than looking to the needs of others (**Philippians 2:3–4**). We must guard our hearts. How do we do that? I would say we guard our hearts the following ways:

- Realize there is a battle for ideas in this world, and that most of the world's thinking is against God (**Romans 12:1–2**). We have to be aware that there is a battle (**Ephesians 6:10–13**). Do not be ignorant of Satan's ways. This will keep us alert rather than just accepting everything we hear.

- Feed on God. We guard our hearts by feeding them the right food. What are you allowing into your life? We have to be careful—**Romans 16:19** says we should be wise about the good and innocent about evil. Feed yourself on the good. Walk away—literally walk away—from bad conversations, bad situations, and unhelpful people.

- Meditate on God. This simply means to stop and take time to think about things that really matter. Let God's thoughts go through your mind (**Philippians 4:8**). After reading a few verses, go back to them through the day. Listen to a sermon and think about what the Bible is really saying. Listen to some praise music and think about what the lyrics really mean. Be strong in the Lord.

Don't be distracted by spiritual activity that does not really matter, like the Pharisees. Commit your mind to God and guard your heart. Jesus called out what was in our hearts. Now we need to replace all that with Him. Be strong in God.

Today we will look at some words of Jesus when He keeps it real. Being His follower is not always an easy thing, but at least Jesus did not hide this fact. The verses we will look at today were originally specifically given to His disciples, but there are some principles here that we can also see apply to this day. First, read **Matthew 10:16–25**.

Who would have thought that someone so peaceful, like Jesus, would have so many enemies? It is amazing to see how many people came against Him when He did not fight anyone. Why? This is important because if people were against Jesus, and we follow Jesus today, then people will be against us also. One reason is pride—if Jesus is God, then we are not. Only one person can truly be in charge of my life—either me or God. A lot of people back then (and today!) want to come to God on their own terms. That is simply evidence of pride. A second reason people did not like Jesus was He reminded them of their own sin, and people like sin, so people avoid those who are doing what is right (**John 3:19–20**). Now we are faced with the reality that if we stand with Jesus, opposition will come (see **2 Timothy 3:12** and **1 Peter 4:12–16**). Matthew 10 gives us a few insights into how we should face opposition.

1. (**10:16**) We are to be wise as serpents when it comes to knowing God. We need to know our stuff. We need to study God's word more and more, so we are wise in these things. But we are also to be as innocent as doves. We do not attack others. We do not argue to win fights but share calmly to win hearts. We need to show how God has changed our lives, so others see that and understand what a great God we follow. We are to be wise and harmless when facing pressure.

2. (**10:17–20**) God will guide and give wisdom. Looking at these verses, notice how it is a fact that we will need to testify why we believe. Today we are not dragged before

leaders of government for our faith like they were, but we have friends who will ask why we are different and changed (hopefully, we are all changing to become more like Christ each day). This can be a little scary—people asking what is up with the change in our life. Jesus tells his disciples to relax and trust Him at those times. God's Holy Spirit will guide us and give us words to say. We can trust God to help us in these moments. Stay close to Him and pray that He will give you wisdom as you go forward in your spiritual life with Him.

3. (**10:21–22**) This is the hard point. It is stating the reality that some people will not like the "new me." Jesus specifically mentions relatives here. Some families do not have a history with God. If you start living with Jesus in your life, some relatives and old friends will not like that. You may be mocked. People might say to you, "What, you think you found Jesus in prison?" or "Don't give me any of that God stuff." We saw from the verses in John 3 above that people don't want to change, but you living a new life forces others to look at their own lives. Many people don't like that. People like their sin, so they don't want some "goody-goody" around them. Now are you ready for that? Are you ready for people to say these things about you? Jesus is clear that these kinds of statements might come from those closest to us. Be ready.

4. (**10:24–25**) Speaking of being ready, Jesus clearly tells us that since He faced opposition, we will too. We are following this guy who got murdered in the end, so we should not be surprised if people come against us today. BUT remember in the face of persecution to be harmless as doves and to trust God's Spirit to lead us. Not only that, but remember how much God sees you and loves you. Jesus says this in **Matthew 10:28–31**. He reminds us that God does care for us and does love us, so do not fear even in the midst of fearful situations. We are valuable in God's eyes. Think about that. Others will disvalue us. Others will tell us we

cannot change—that we will fail. Others will tell us that we are too far gone. Others will tell us that no one cares about us. All of these are Satan's lies. God loves us very much and values us. That is why even when we are facing opposition and people who are against God, we can have peace and joy. The next time people discourage you, remember God and look to Him. Keep Him in front of you because He sees you and has you in His hand.

Have you ever followed the directions to put something together, and in the end, it didn't work? You flipped that switch after doing all you were supposed to, and…nothing. Sometimes "some assembly required" means "good luck with this." I wonder how God looks at our lives. I would think He gets frustrated with us since He assembled us, did everything right, and even gave us His own instruction manual—the Bible. It is our guidebook, and God does His part, but then we do not do our part, and we are broken. Why do we wind up broken? A lot of times, we know what to do. The problem is not with our knowledge, but our problem is we do not follow through with what we know to do. Jesus talked about this in **Luke 6:46–49**. Take a moment to read those verses.

Jesus compares two men here, one wise and one foolish. Obviously, a house needs a strong foundation, and we should not build on sand. So what is the difference between the two men? Notice that both men actually hear God's word. They both listen to Jesus! That is great, but one of them does not change his life and does not actually do what he heard. So the foolish man listened and never changed, while the wise man listened and lived differently; he lived according to the words he heard. This is the main issue—not even whether we are listening to God or not, but are we actually applying what we hear from God into our lives? Are we living out what Jesus is teaching? That is true wisdom.

A lot of people are just hearers these days. People go to church, listen (sort of), and never change. Even I can find myself reading God's word but forgetting what I have read or just go through times of life where I am not working on something spiritually. Jesus is pretty clear here—if you are putting yourself in places to hear God's word or even reading God's word yourself and are not changing anything in your life, then you are a fool. That sounds harsh, but those are not my words. Jesus says here we are fools if we do not do what God says. Sometimes we do not follow through with doing because we are not paying attention;

sometimes we don't really want to change—changing is hard! But that is what Jesus is saying here. When He says to do His word, this means we are living life, read something in His word, and now put that new action or attitude into practice. We are changing, and that is being wise!

So how do we do this? How do we do this doing? First, we need to be active listeners. This means when I hear a preacher, I really focus. This means when I read the Bible, I really slow down and think about what I am reading. The goal is to get one thought to take with me through the day (and each day this week). That will now be the spiritual goal I have for myself during the week ahead.

For example, read **Luke 6:32–36**. These verses tell us to be merciful and giving, even to those who are not kind back to us. Now we can blow past these verses in our reading, especially since we think we are pretty good and treat others well. But what we should do is take that word *merciful* and keep it going through our minds over the next few days. We need to remind ourselves of these verses. But we haven't actually done anything new yet—wait for it. Then a few days from now, some jerk on the block might ask to borrow something from you. You don't like this guy, and he might not return it anyway, so you really want to say no. But these verses come back to you at this moment, and you remember Luke 6:34. If you say no to this guy, you are like everyone else. If you say yes, you are a lot more like Jesus. Now you might say, "But then he is going to take my stuff." Maybe. But what would Jesus do? You see, this is where it becomes hard to actually follow God's word, but we need to—it is better for us and others. We are gaining character through this process. We are learning the value of other people through this—because God values other people. It is wise to read these verses and do them.

I don't know where you are at with your relationship with God, but I know He wants all of us to be followers of Him who are changing and living out the verses we read. This is not easy. Reading and forgetting is easy. Reading and doing is hard. Today, try to see what one idea God is showing you—think about it and keep it close in your mind so you can do it. Be wise, like Jesus says.

Day 10   **Jesus (Part 8)**   Luke 14

Today, we will look at some tough words by Jesus. As you know, I appreciate that He really wanted to keep it real for us. When we come to Him, He offers us internal peace, joy, purpose for living, and eternity with Him. But He is also clear that outer peace here on earth is not coming. By turning to Jesus, we will find that not everyone will be happy for us; we may even find more conflict. As we have said before, the reason people reject Jesus is because when we accept Jesus, we admit we cannot save ourselves—many people, like the Pharisees in the Bible, would rather think that they are better than others and don't need saving and don't need Jesus. They are offended at the cross and upset with us—we don't join in their activities anymore; we don't want to have their kind of "fun" anymore. This can create conflict, and we need to be ready to stand for God. Read **Luke 14:25–33**. What do you think Jesus is saying here? What do you think verse 33 means for us today?

It is interesting that in verse 25, Jesus has great crowds following Him—and it is almost like He doesn't want so big a crowd. The reason for this is that Jesus knows not everyone in the crowd is sincere. Not everyone there is understanding what following Jesus is really all about. There is a good book out there titled *Not a Fan* by Kyle Idleman. We like being fans of sports teams—we cheer and identify with the team, but we don't actually sacrifice anything to join the team or do any of the exercise. We see the team on TV and cheer, but we did not do any of the work they put in to be good at their sport. Too many people are just fans of Jesus. We take a few of His sayings and put them on our wall. When times are tough, we pray. When times are good, we say thanks, and that is that. Our lives don't really change; we just add Jesus to our fan page.

Jesus was not calling for us to join a crowd and once a week cheer for Him. He does not need more fans. He is calling us to an entire life change. Look at what he says:

- (verse 26) You need to love me more than your family. If your family says it is us or Jesus, you need to be ready to choose Jesus.
- (verse 27) You need to bear your own cross. If you follow Jesus, life will become hard, and you need to be ready for that. Stay with Him through hard times.
- (verse 28–32) Don't quit on Jesus. Don't join and turn back when it gets hard. Go all in.
- (verse 33) You have to follow Jesus above everything else in your life.

These are interesting words because it is like He is chasing away the crowd by scaring them. But it is not fear—it is reality of this sinful world. Jesus wants to know if you are serious about Him. He does not want you to be just a fan, but He wants you to be an active participant in being His disciple. He must be the purpose for which we live. Besides, if we don't go all in with Him, how do we expect to change as people? Jesus is not a good-luck charm, and He is not a genie in a bottle to give us our wishes. He is THE purpose for life because He is the only way out of this sinful world. Are you ready to truly follow Him?

Now, can I say this about verse 33? Jesus wants us to let go of everything this world offers in exchange for Him. In one sense, that sounds harsh—I have to release *everything* in this life? Yes. But remember this: **God wants our all because nothing we have is as good as the life He is offering**. Think about that. This world offers a lot—but the end of sin is a miserable life. It is fun for a while but always ends badly (see **Proverbs 14:12**). God loves us more than that. He knows that life with Him is better than what this world offers. So He asks for our all, since that is what is best for us. If we are holding on to some things from this world, then we are not 100 percent with Jesus.

Where are you at? Are you just trying Jesus out? Are you 50 percent with God and 50 percent with this world? That doesn't work. How about 99 percent with Jesus? That also doesn't work. What is that 1 percent you won't give to Him? He is trustworthy. Don't be afraid. If God takes something from you, it is because He has something better for your future. You may not see it now, but that is what faith is. In *all* your ways, acknowledge Him, and He will direct your paths! **Proverbs 3:5–6**. Let yourself truly be one of His followers. Let us be Jesus's disciples today. May God give you strength.

Today, I want to do something a little different. I want you to share thoughts with yourself, or if you read this with someone else, then go over the questions together or share as a group. I will share a passage for us to read and give a few questions for us to think about. Really think about them. Tomorrow, I will comment on these ideas, but challenge yourself to take some time and really meditate about what God might be saying to you through these verses.

Our passage today is **Luke 9:46–62**. There are actually four sections here. Read and see below:

1. **Luke 9:46–48**. Think about what is happening. The disciples are arguing about who is greatest—and they are discussing this in the presence of Jesus! Jesus does not scold them but rather sits a child among them and teaches. That is probably not what we would do to a bunch of arguers, but He wanted to get their attention.
   - What do you think is a good definition of *greatness* according to Jesus?
   - Why do you think accepting a child is so important to following Jesus?
   - What are some ways you can be *great* in Jesus's eyes, seeing what he said in verse 48?
2. **Luke 9:49–50**
   - Why do you think the disciples were concerned about stopping this other person?
   - What do you think Jesus is telling us about others here?
3. **Luke 9:51–56**. In these verses, we must remember that Samaritans hated the Jews (Jesus and His disciples), and Jews hated Samaritans. We know Jesus continued to try to reach the Samaritans anyway (**John 4**), but we see here

that His disciples were looking to punish Samaritans pretty quickly and severely.

- How do you think the disciples felt when they were rejected by the Samaritans?
- Why do you think Jesus felt differently? How do you think He felt?
- What does this mean for us today?

4. **Luke 9:57–62.** This is a famous passage where Jesus addresses a few men who wanted to follow Him but not fully. Remember that in the context of the passage and time back then, burying the father meant many days of ceremonies (and some theologians believe the father was not even dead yet, but it was being used as an excuse to delay following Jesus for years). Also, the last man's farewell would be a much bigger deal than packing and saying goodbye. It also would be a ceremony of many days. So Jesus is making clear about where He should be in our priorities.

- Why do you think these three guys did not follow Jesus in the end?
- Why do you think Jesus basically scared them off?
- What does Jesus really mean in these verses? What does it mean to truly follow Jesus?
- What then does truly following Jesus mean to you specifically in your life?

These are really important verses. Take some time to think and go through the questions. I will comment on the questions tomorrow, but let God's Spirit guide you in thinking through what these verses mean to you and what God is teaching you today. This is a great way to dig deeper into God's Word. May He bless and guide.

Yesterday, you looked at questions about **Luke 9:46–62**. I trust God blessed your time thinking about these verses. I have thought about the passage as well and will comment on the questions. These are just my thoughts and not the "right answers." My insight is limited, but there is benefit in sharing together like this.

1. **Luke 9:46–48**
   - Jesus defined greatness as being the "least" among a crowd. This is the opposite of the world's definition. This shows greatness is helping others and serving others rather than being served.
   - I think Jesus brought in a child because a child cannot give us anything back. If I am kind to a child, I will not get status or money or favors in return. Jesus wants us to care for others without thinking of what we can get from that relationship. This is true greatness—helping because there is a need and not because I can get some benefit back from being kind.
   - We all need to be looking for people we can minister to and help. The poorer and weaker the person, the more help they need, and the more we should be helping. We can be practical with our time and money. We all have time to give to others.

2. **Luke 9:49–50**
   - I think the disciples were concerned about being the highest in status, and here was someone else who said he was working for Jesus. Ultimately, they wanted the top spot in Jesus's world and not have to compete with others for that position.
   - Jesus wants us to get along and not be concerned about our status so much. The other person was not spreading false teaching, so Jesus wanted his disciples

to be accepting of Him. Sometimes, just listening to others and accepting them is a humble act we can do for people.

3. **Luke 9:51–56**

- I think the disciples were offended the Samaritans did not accept them and wanted revenge. Since it was a Samaritan village, they were pretty quick to judge and not eager to give them any extra time for repentance.
- Jesus clearly felt differently. He had compassion on the Samaritans. I think He knew this was not the time to go to them—they were not ready or willing. That was sad, but someday their hearts might turn. Jesus did not come to punish people—He came to patiently wait for people to come to Him and accept the free gift of life (**Romans 6:23**) that He was offering. He was hoping someday these Samaritans would change. This is how He feels about us as well; He is always rooting for us to change. God's judgment is sure but is also His last resort.
- Today, this means we need to be willing to wait for others; we need to patiently present Jesus to others even if they do not accept today. We pray that they would get right with God right now. There is no place for revenge. We may need to walk away but at the same time pray that God would still work.

4. **Luke 9:57–62**

- I think these guys wanted an easy faith. They wanted Jesus in word but not in reality. They wanted the easy path to faith.
- Jesus is not interested in fakers who say one thing but live another. Jesus wants us to be real.
- To truly follow Jesus means a life change. A couple days ago, I mentioned that God wants our all because what He is offering is better than anything we have. He wants to give us new life, but we need to be ready

to give our lives to Him for that to happen. We need to be all in.

I hope you are truly following Jesus. Sometimes we are not sure if we are ready or able to follow that strongly, but it starts with just one step today of acknowledging Him in your life. He will guide. We just need to do the next right thing, whatever that is, and trust that God will guide the fallout—because He will. There is no better life than being fully with God. Don't miss it because you held on to something or someone that kept you from God.

Today, take a look at **Mark 1:29–39**. What are a few things you notice from here? Is there anything we can learn from Jesus from these verses (of course there is!)?

First, look at what happened here. Jesus heals Simon's mother-in-law, and as word spreads, many people come for healing. At this time in history, there seemed to be a lot of demon activity (perhaps because of Jesus's presence), so He heals and casts out demons. He does this a lot. He is probably tired, but Jesus gets up early the next day—really early (while it was still dark)—and goes off alone to pray. As people wake up, they look for Jesus, and finally some disciples find Him. They tell Jesus that everyone is looking for Him, but He does not go back to that town. Instead, he goes into new towns to preach. I think there are two really big ideas here that we can take away from these verses.

A. Time with God (prayer)

Wow, how important was prayer and time alone with God to Jesus? It was so important that after such a busy day, Jesus still got up super early the next morning so He could have time alone with God. This is a big challenge to us. I know that I cannot say I spend enough time in prayer. I fall short in this area, and it seems to be really important. So let's see how we can be like Jesus in prayer.

1. Set aside time. Jesus knew He would have a busy day—He made time. Some people are morning people and some are night people—doesn't matter. Get some time, morning or night, that you can dedicate to God.

2. Alone. We all need that time where it is just God and us. During that time, we can pray, read His word, or even just take a few verses and really think about them (**Psalm 1:2**). That is meditation—thinking deeply about something.

Meditate on God, a verse, His truth, and where you are heading in life. Take time to refocus your life on Him.

3. Prayer. Jesus gave us a model for prayer in **Matthew 6:9–13**. Based on the Lord's prayer, we can say these are the parts of prayer: Spend time praising God. Spend time praying for yourself—ask God to guide your life and grow you in Him. Share your questions. God can handle it. Ask requests, but more than that, ask for God's will to be done. He knows what is best. Pray for others and for their spiritual needs above all. You may even want to write out your prayer. That is a discipline that many find helpful. Writing down a prayer forces us to take time to think about exactly what we are praying. This sounds easy but can actually be hard. This is what the psalms are—written prayers. **Psalm 32 and 34** are examples. I would even challenge you to take some time this weekend to write out a prayer. God knows you, loves you, and wants to hear from you.

B. Care for others

The other lesson in this Mark 1 passage is the care that Jesus had for others. It would have been easy for Him to just stay in that one village—He was popular there. They loved Him and were looking for Him. Why start all over? But he started over because there were other villages that needed to hear. God is not about our comfort. He is going to keep us comfortable for eternity after this life is over, but right now He wants to use us to reach people (**2 Corinthians 5:18–20**). Jesus packed up His followers and moved on because it was best for those other people. God wants to teach you things about Him—then He wants you to go tell others. Some of you do have opportunities to share with others about God—do it. Share with kindness and gentleness, but share. May others know that you are a true follower of Christ. That is the challenge before us—and we need God's strength, which comes through prayer. Jesus prayed and then went to work. May this be a day of prayer for all of us in preparation for what God has for us next. Great verses here. May God bless and guide.

Day 14   **Jesus (Part 12)**   John 1:14

Today is the last day in this series, but we will go to a verse at the beginning of Jesus's earthly life because it summarizes who Jesus truly is and why he came. Look at **John 1:14**. This is Jesus Christ. He is the very Word of God in human form. Why? So that we could see His glory—the glory of God. Let's think about what this verse means and how that affects us.

1. Never forget who Jesus is. He is God. He said so and actually showed it, unlike others throughout history who have made that claim. The phrase "dwelt among us" is very personal. He came to mix with us and to be known by us. We humans that have come after His time have detailed records of His life in Matthew, Mark, Luke, and John. It says we beheld, or saw, His glory—the glory of God. Jesus came as the Son of God so we could understand the relationship He has with God. Jesus is God. God is one God in three persons (hard for our human minds to grasp, yet true). Jesus was and is one with God (**John 1:1–3**), but while He was here on earth, He was physically separate from God the Father (**Philippians 2:6–8**). He was separate, but still very close in relationship, just like a father and son. We beheld that glory of God. He showed us how to live by showing how God would live on earth. He showed us love, not just by saying He loved us, but by going to the cross for us. He wanted us to have no doubt about the love of God for us. Look at **John 1:12**. Because of Jesus, if we believe, God enables us to enter a relationship with Him. We become children adopted into God's family. Wow. What an honor! This is a truth we can see Jesus taught in His ministry. But in verse 14, it also says Jesus was full of grace and truth. What is the truth about us and God? What is grace? Let's see.

2. In the Old Testament, God was helping us understand that we are sinners. That is the truth. God sometimes dealt very harshly with sin in the OT. Why? It was so we could understand how holy God is and how sinful we are. Actually, most OT characters/prophets we read about have sin problems too. They were men like us, while God is still holy. Our sin puts us in a bad spot. Jesus showed this truth when He was on earth, and many people did not like Him for that (**John 3:19–20**). What can be done? How can we as sinners go to a holy God? We have no right to go to Him (**Romans 3:23, 6:23**). All of this is truth, which shows we really need God's grace. Good news—Jesus is full of grace too.

3. The truth is that since we are sinners, we needed help, so Jesus paid our sin penalty on the cross. He wanted to allow us to come to God, even though we are sinners, as well as set an example of selfless love and grace. Now we need to think about the impact of this grace. This grace allows us to go to God after this life because when we accept Jesus, God sees our sin paid for (**Romans 3:23–26**). But this grace also enables us to restart and live life for Him right now (**Romans 8:1**). This is living by grace, and it is a concept that is so powerful. I was listening to a sermon a couple days ago, and I stopped when I heard this quote: "None of us is where we should be...but every one of us can start where we are" (Mark Driscoll). That is the power of God's grace! Without Jesus, how can we get to God and how can we ever change our lives? We can't. We all need forgiveness and grace. So grace says that wherever we are, we can draw a line and start over. That is so freeing! We do not need to pay for our past; Jesus did. Go forward in God! God wants to take us forward from wherever we are—we need to let Him. Now some people abuse God's grace—they say, "I will just live like I want and ask forgiveness later." God does not approve of that (**Romans 6:1–2**)—this is why grace is dangerous, but God is willing to take that risk for us. He is

willing to take us as we are and let us restart. Don't waste His grace. Take advantage of the new life we have in Him.

So in light of who Jesus is and why He came (to give us full and abundant life, **John 10:10**), what are you doing with another chance? That is God's grace—another chance. God came and lived among us so we could see His heart for us. Talk is cheap, so Jesus came to show us God's love for real. John 1:14 is such a huge verse that summarizes life for us. Live in His grace. Go forward in Him. Always remember the truth of who we are (undeserving) and the truth of God's grace (loves us anyway).

Day 15   2 Peter 1 (Part 1)

Start today by reading **2 Peter 1:1–15**. What stands out to you? What do you think is the purpose of these verses that Peter wrote to other believers (like us)? How can these verses help us today?

A. Read verses 1–2 again

1. Peter says that other people's faith is "of equal standing" with his. This is actually an amazing statement. Your faith and relationship with God is just as important to God as Peter's was even, though he was clearly special as a disciple and preacher of God. Wow! We are that valuable to God. Jesus never looked at some people as better than others since we all need Him. God doesn't look at us differently— He loves each of us so much and values our faith—every one of us. This fact really helps us see who we are and how our identity is in Christ, the One who truly loves us.

2. Verse 2 seems to say that the ability to live in grace and peace increases with more knowledge of God and Jesus Christ. How do you think this is true? I think that the more we learn about who Jesus was and how He lived here on earth, the more we can show God's grace to others. As we grow in knowledge about God's holiness and yet also love to us, we understand His grace more deeply. This allows us to be gracious to others and brings about deeper peace in our life in the midst of difficulties. Remember, in the midst of struggles, we can always know the end of the story with Christ—we will not find our peace on this earth; rather, it is focusing on an eternity with the one who loves us so much. Read **2 Corinthians 4:16–18**. What are those verses saying? I love those verses. I think they acknowledge that this life brings us affliction, but we can still rest in His "eternal weight of glory." This is being with God in peace

forever—not because of me but because of Him (**Romans 5:8**). These are all facts that are so important since we might look at the story of our life right now as a pretty sad or broken book. In Christ, your story can have a happy ending, but you need to pour yourself into knowing God better and better.

B.   Read 2 Peter 1:3–5 again

1.   Really think about that phrase in verse 3, "[A]ll things that pertain to life and godliness." This is saying that God has given us all we need for life and living a godly life here and now while we wait to be with Him in eternity. That means the Bible has our answers for life. This means we can trust God's leading in our life. This means we can choose to honor God in our life, and the result of that will be better than if we ignore God. I recently read in a magazine a songwriter saying that addiction and debt are two things that enslave us in this world. Think about that. This world offers us escape through things (alcohol, drugs, big things money can buy even if we don't have that money now) that really enslave us to them. Enslave. Like we no longer control ourselves, and our desire for this stuff controls us. We become obsessed and focused on things that do not lead to a full life. God knows we can experience life fully in grace and peace through Him. He does not want us to be enslaved to sin but make right choices. We need to increase in the knowledge of Him in order to make those right choices that lead to "excellence" (His word in verse 3). The key to this happening is increasing in the knowledge of God through Jesus Christ.

2.   Verse 4 reminds us that God wants to help us escape the corruption of this world. I think we all know that we live in a broken world. This world has been made corrupt by sinful desire. We naturally desire to make choices that are sinful and not good for us. These wrong choices lead to a

bad end—even though some things are fun in the moment. God is offering us a better way to live now as well as permanent delivery from any effects of sin. Through Jesus, he took care of all that for us.

3. So now He says that whole process of changing your life begins with faith (verse 5) and continues with living out your faith. We will cover that next time. But for now, consider the gift of God: that through faith alone, He offers us freedom from enslaving desires and sin's power, as well as eternity with Him. Wow! If you have never started your journey of faith with God, he offers that freedom from sin to you now. Talk to Him (**Ephesians 2:8–9, Romans 6:23, Hebrews 10:19–23, 1 Peter 1:3–5**).

Day 16   2 Peter 1 (Part 2)

Start off by reading **2 Peter 1:1–15** again. What do you remember from yesterday about the first five verses? As we start today, the next verses are about living here on earth now even though we are looking to heaven in the future. Verse 4 reminds us of those promises of being with God, but we are still in this corrupt world. God shows us a better way to live through the next few verses.

A.   Faith

What is faith? Read **Hebrews 11:1–6**. Faith is action based on agreeing with God that he exists and that we need Him. This list in 2 Peter begins with faith. Why is that important? Remember, it is not our good works that begin a relationship with God. It is faith in Him (that's all!) and agreeing with Him that our works are worthless to a holy God. Paul talked about how he had done so many spiritual things but found them worthless compared to God. That is true faith! Read **Philippians 3:3–10**.

B.   Virtue

Virtue is faith lived out. Once we understand who Jesus is and how much He loves us as we are, we want to live life for Him to show Him to the rest of the world. This good living (virtue) is not so we can be worthy of Him (we are not). It is because He already accepted us and is showing us a better way to live while we remain on earth. Read **2 Corinthians 5:14–15**. The more I understand His love, the more it controls me and allows me to live for Him. This is the best way to live for my own benefit AND the benefit of others since I will be showing love to them.

C.   Knowledge

I need to add knowledge to my faith. I do not need to know everything when I come to God. I just need to put my faith in Him. But once I do that, it is a good idea to get to know God, my Savior, better. This is increasing in knowledge—knowing Him better. Maybe you remember first being interested in a girl. You could not get enough time with her. You were giving your own time to her by investing in this relationship. God wants us to know Him. Invest time in that relationship with Him. He is worth it.

D. Self-control

Self-control is needed for many reasons. It is needed so we stay on the right path and needed so we can focus each day on what is right. It is also like the self-control we need to do daily exercise. What spiritual exercise can you do each day to stay close to God at this time? I would say be sure to pray each day for yourself to grow in God, for your family on the outside, and for those around you now. Also, be sure to spend some time in God's Word or reading spiritual books. This mental discipline leads to self-control in actions toward those who annoy us. Jesus was patient. We need that now.

E. Steadfastness

Not every day will be easy. Actually, most will be hard. Stick with it, though. Always do the next right thing no matter how little difference it seems to make in tough times. Read **1 Peter 4:12–14.**

F. Godliness

This is like virtue—it is living a life that looks like Jesus. We say we are following Him. Live like Him.

G. Brotherly affection and love

This is what the love of God looks like shown through us. What is love? How does God show that he loves us? How do we show our love for God? Read **John 13:34–35** for the answer. We show love for God by showing love to others. How are you doing with that? We usually think of what others are doing for us. This is why Jesus was radical—he thought of how we can care for others first.

What do we do with this list from 2 Peter 1? Think about which characteristic above you need to work on the most. Work on it. Pray each day that you would grow in that area. Remember, we can always summarize this whole thing with a focus on knowledge and love. Memorize some verses. Increase in knowledge. Also, love others. Always respond with love to others even if they do not deserve it. We will come through the next few weeks either better at showing God's love or worse at showing it. Remember how much God loves you.

Day 17   2 Peter 1 (Part 3)

Introduction: How does one show that he is a follower of Jesus Christ? What does that life look like? How does the world we live in distract people from following Jesus? Think about it. The main part of this chapter is verses 5–7 and the qualities listed, which we can grow in. We covered those last time but review them now. Next, read **2 Peter 1:8–9**. What do you think these verses are saying?

A.   Living it out (verse 8)

By working on these qualities in our lives (faith, virtue, knowledge, self-control, steadfastness, godliness, love), we show that we know Jesus. Jesus is not about keeping rules; He is about love and compassion to others. These characteristics in our lives show that we know and understand Him. This verse says that by growing in these qualities, we will not be "ineffective" as people. We will be growing and fruitful/successful people. God writes these verses to help us know Him because the world is a better place when people are living out their faith in God.

Here is an example. Read **Luke 19:1–10**. Zacchaeus cheated people. What did Jesus say in verse 5? Did Jesus say Zacchaeus needed to not be a sinner and then Jesus would visit him? Did Jesus say to start keeping the law and then He would visit? No, Jesus needed to visit him today so that Zacchaeus could see who Jesus was. Once Zacchaeus saw Jesus for real, he changed (v. 8). His outward act of paying back those he cheated was evidence he understood and accepted Jesus (vv. 9–10). When our heart is changed, people will notice. They will see self-control, steadfastness, godliness, and love. The more we get to know Jesus, the easier it will be for us to live for Him.

B. Not living it out (verse 9)

Back in 2 Peter, we see a statement about someone who is not changing. If we are not becoming more like Jesus in these areas, a big reason is that we forgot what we were saved from. We forget how bad sin is, which leads us back to where we came from. Read **Proverbs 26:11**—this describes those returning to their former sin. Peter talks about how the world wants to enable us to return to our past sin! Read **2 Peter 2:17–22**. What stands out to you? Verse 19 stands out to me. The world tells us to be free, follow our heart, and do whatever we want. Yet so much sin that is tempting to us leads us to be enslaved (addicted) to it. God wants us to follow the qualities in 1:5–7 because He knows they will lead to freedom from sin's power in our daily lives. They are the gospel of Jesus lived out, living like He did. If we forget to move our life toward Jesus, we will be in danger of returning to sins which want to enslave us.

Telling us to live in self-control, godliness, and love sounds like a harder way to live than just doing what we want. But no! God loves us so much and knows that we will be enslaved to what the world offers. Trust Him and live for Him—it is so much better for us. You will "never fail" if you follow this path (verses 10–11) because God is leading us to His eternal kingdom. And as you can see in **Ephesians 2:8–9**, God offers us this new freeing (not enslaving) life for free, as a gift based on His grace. Wow!

C. Help each other (2 Peter 1:12–15)

Peter is writing these words to these believers because he wants them to be "established in the truth" and to never forget. We need reminders (v. 13). A walk with God is very daily. Each day, we need to be reminded of the gospel (**John 3:16**) and set our mind on Him for today. Peter wanted to remind these people of that, and so too we can encourage and uplift each other every day. What do you need to do to remember God each day? When we stay in Him daily, we can be a follower of Christ who is encouraging others—one who is a light to others (**Matthew 5:14–16**). Freely we have received from Him, freely may we give to others. Have a blessed day.

Day 18   2 Peter 3

As the days go by, always fix your hope on Jesus. Today, 2 Peter 3 is such a good chapter of the Bible with a few major thoughts for us—these thoughts are actually touching on some pretty deep issues, like purpose of living. First, read **2 Peter chapter 3**.

A. Now read verses 1–7 again. What do you think these verses are saying? Who are scoffers?

Scoffers come along and mock what you believe—in this case, they mock our faith. They do this two ways in these verses—they say God is not coming again, and they ignore God's role in the earth being here today. Sound familiar? This describes the world we live in today. People want to say that there is no God at all. Notice the reason that scoffers mock God—the root of it is because they are "following their own sinful desires." People always are looking for an excuse to follow their own sinful desires. We all do this to some extent (How do we make excuses for sin in our own lives? Think about it). One of the biggest excuses in the world is, "There is no God, so I can do what I want. Don't tell me what to do." That is what is happening here in 2 Peter 3, and God answers their scoffing in the following verses.

B. In verses 8–10, God says He is not ending time yet because He does not want anyone to die (perish). To Him, one thousand years is nothing. He is being patient. He loves us! He does not want to come back at a time when not many people are trusting Him. He wants His word spread as much as possible for our own good so as many people as possible have a chance with God. Technology is advancing, and more people than ever can hear the gospel with just a click on their computer or phone. But verse 10 reminds us He is also holy, and His patience will not last forever.

He made the earth, and He will end it also. So when we are confronted with people like this (vv. 1–7), do not get angry. Be like God and be patient toward them, praying for their repentance. God loves them.

C. That brings us to the HUGE application lesson of this chapter. Read verses 11–18 again. What do you think the big lesson is for us? It is pretty clear in verse 11: what we do for this life on earth will not last, so what kind of person should you be in what really matters, specifically holiness and godliness? If at the end of our life and the end of this earth we will meet God, then we should live with that in mind all the time. That is what really matters. Look at verse 14. How can we be found without sin and at peace with God? It is only through Jesus Christ. Read **Colossians 1:19–23** and **Romans 5:1–2**. Until God comes again, count His patience (v. 15) as a blessing to allow us time to get right with Him and share His message with others.

By the way, notice in verse 16 that Peter admits some of Paul's writing (many books in the New Testament) is hard to understand. That is why we need others to talk with about God's Word when we don't understand, but it is also comforting to know that we are not the first ones to ever find parts of the Bible hard. That being said, also notice in verses 16–17 how some people purposely try to twist Scripture to match what they want it to say—may we never do that or listen to those who twist God's Word. Instead, keep growing in the knowledge of God—it says this in verse 18. Grow in grace and knowledge. Grow in knowledge by studying His word more, like we are doing right now. Grow in grace by resting in God and His grace to you, while showing God's grace to others each day.

Closing questions: What are you living for? Part of the way to answer that is where do you see yourself ten years from now? What role will God play in your future life? Also, on a smaller scale but still important, how are you planning on growing in the knowledge of God? What are some ways to do that? How can you grow in the grace of God now? What are ways and opportunities to show the grace of God to others? Be careful—it is really hard to show grace and be a gracious person. But God calls us to grow in His grace and show it to the world. May God encourage you today in realizing how gracious He is to you. As we grow in that understanding, may God's grace live through us.

Day 19   Galatians 5:13–26 (Part 1)

I have been thinking about these verses lately, so we will take the next few days and work our way through them. First, read **Galatians 5:13–26** once or twice. Secondly, take a mental note or actually write down three big ideas that stick out to you from these verses. Also, what do you think is the most challenging idea or command from these verses? Today, we will just look at the first few verses in detail.

Galatians 5:13–15: You are free…to love others.

So what does this whole freedom thing mean? Does it mean I am free to do whatever I want, and God is fine with it? No. We kind of need to back up a bit and see the context. Most of Galatians is explaining about how we are free from the Old Testament law (read **2:15–16**) since we are saved by faith. So let's think about that for a minute. Many religions around the world require you to do certain things, like pray at a certain time or in a certain way, or to burn incense to an idol at a specific time that is important (usually dictated by the moon), or recite certain creeds or prayers a specific number of times, or wear a special set of clothes. Why? All of these are followed in other religions because these acts get us points with God. We then need a certain number of points (usually pretty unknown) in order to get to heaven. We are getting God to love us more by what we do. And Paul writes to the Galatians, NO! You do NOT get God to love you more by doing things or get "points" in order to get to heaven by works (read **3:1–14**). In chapter 5, we see the big work that the Galatians wanted to do was circumcision (ouch!). They thought they could get God to accept them more if they were circumcised. The apostle Paul gets quite upset at this teaching (see **5:1–12**).

That brings us back to this idea of freedom. We are free in Christ from rituals and spending time, making sure that we have the right clothes and the right words for prayers or do everything at the exact right time. We are free from all that worry—great! So what do we do with our extra free time God gave us? We love others! We are free from rituals so we can have more time to care for others and help others out. We are free from the law so we can give ourselves to others (**5:14**). Wait—are we then free to party and do what we want? No. That is why verse 13 says to not use this freedom as an opportunity to do what is wrong and please your flesh. That will get us going down a wrong road in life that will actually lead us away from freedom and back into slavery to sin (**Romans 6:6–18**). Once we start going down the path of a certain sin, it only becomes easier and easier to do that sin again. God wants us to use this freedom to help others rather than helping ourselves to sin.

There is a problem in helping others and loving others—it involves other people. I mean, some people are just pretty unlovable. Then there are people who just take advantage of my kindness and never pay me back. There are so many selfish people out there that I better look out for myself. And yet this verse says the whole law is summarized in loving others as myself. Jesus said to love our enemies and those who persecute us (**Matthew 5:43–48**). Look, loving others is the best option in life. Why? In verse 15, it shows the opposite of love and describes it as biting and devouring each other. What do you think that means? Think about it a minute.

That is what we do to each other. We do bite at each other in our comments about people we don't like or people we want to push down so they stay behind us. In the end, we devour others, so we are ahead of people in popularity and attention. I want to be king of my kingdom, and it leads to everyone being "consumed by one another." That is the ironic thing—when we push down others and disregard others, it will come back on us. What goes around comes around (not a Bible verse, but still). God is offering us a better way. He says to us, "I have freed you from worrying about keeping rituals and memorizing prayers that must be said in a certain way. You are free from laws about exactly how to do worship. But you are free so you can take that extra time to really think about how to show love to your neighbor." Remember, our neighbor is whoever we happen to be around at any time. We are free—free from the power of sin in Jesus so that we can love others. Have a great day.

Day 20   Galatians 5:13–26 (Part 2)

Yesterday we looked at the first few verses here. Read the passage again to review. Today I want to focus on verses **16–21**. As you read those verses specifically, what stands out to you and what "works of the flesh" from the list do you see in your life? We all can find some issues here.

A. Spirit vs. Flesh (vv. 16–18)

These verses acknowledge that we have a battle in this life—it is with our flesh (what we want to do) against the Spirit (what we should do). This battle is a big one and also explained in **Romans 7:14–23**. I think the main thing here is to know that as long as we are on earth, we will have to fight ourselves. We need to feed the Spirit to fight against our flesh because whatever we feed will be stronger. The Spirit is from God, whom we receive when we accept Jesus. We can spend time with God and train our mind to pray and remember God's Word throughout the day. That takes work. That means setting aside time to study God's word. That means listening to music or videos of speakers that are talking about God and praising God. Our mind naturally just wants to find what is easy or pleasurable, even if it is not good for us. We must acknowledge that what we "feel" like doing is usually the opposite of what we should do and what God wants us to do. God will help us, but we need to be ready to fight against ourselves.

B. The specific areas of battle (vv. 19–21)

Well, now we come to a list. This list defines for us what these "works of the flesh" are. These are characteristics of people who do not know Jesus. Sometimes followers of Jesus fall in these areas also, but these are sins that followers of Jesus will actively fight against in their life. We can all find ourselves in this list—we are different people and have different weaknesses, but we have them. Sometimes we look down on people who do something, only because we don't do that, but we have a different area that causes us to stumble. So there should be no pride when we don't do something on this list, but only humility and gratefulness that God has helped us conquer an area. Overall, we should study the list and really target areas for spiritual battles in our lives. Be real with yourself.

Looking at the list, there seem to be two big areas of fleshly desires. The first one is sexual immorality. It is mentioned in the list along with impurity, sensuality, "drunkenness, orgies and things like those." This world says do what you want; don't let anyone tell you that you are wrong. But the reality is that God's way of one man and one woman is best for us and our kids. The road to a free sex weekend is paved with broken hearts and broken lives. It is not that God doesn't want us to have sex; it is that God wants us to enjoy it in the context of marriage. These are words that sound old-fashioned in the world today but ring true in reality. The world makes it easy to fall in this area with all its messages that say, "It's just sex; everyone does it" (have you heard modern music?), but God knows this leads our hearts away from Him. Don't play with the fire of immorality. (Read **Proverbs 6:27–32 and all of Proverbs chapter 7**.)

The second big area listed is division—enmity, strife, rivalries, dissentions, divisions—which is started by internal feelings of jealousy, envy, and fits of anger. Wow. Our flesh is naturally only interested in ourselves. When other people get in our way or have success that we do not, we get angry or jealous. This leads us to telling people how bad they are so that I look good. Here come divisions. People don't get along because we hold on to past arguments or jealousies and never forgive. Hey, the reality is that people are different, and some will bother us a lot or even sin against us. If we hold on to those hurts forever, there will only be division, strife, and fighting. Followers of Jesus should be the leaders in loving and forgiving each other and promoting unity. Remember, it starts on the inside with taking the feelings of anger and envy and giving them over to God. He will protect you. Then we can focus on healing broken relationships and being peacemakers as Jesus was (**Matthew 5:9**).

I do not know where you are on this list, but if you have failed in a few areas, welcome to the club. The key is asking God's forgiveness and pushing forward. That is God's grace. He wants us to be renewed in Christ. Fighting against our flesh is a real battle, but don't give up. God will help and show us a better way to live through Jesus. Be strong in Him.

Day 21   Galatians 5:13–26 (Part 3)

Last time we got through verse 21 and saw a few troubling areas that our flesh goes to which are against God. The good news is God's grace is bigger, and He wants so much more for us. Specifically, He wants us to rest in His Spirit and focus on Him so that we can bear fruit. Read **Galatians 5:22–23**. What a list! This is the fruit of the Spirit of God. We are going to see each fruit individually, but first a few things about them:

1. Fruit takes time to get ripe. If you plant a tree, time is needed for it to grow and mature and get to the point that it bears fruit. It is the same in our life—be patient and let God change you.
2. A tree needs watering to grow and bear fruit. That is also the same with us. We cannot grow in the fruit of the Spirit if we are not feeding ourselves on the things of God. Jesus said it well in **John 15:4–5**. We must continue to feed on the things of God in order to change our thinking and life patterns to become more like Jesus. Think about what you can do to help you think about God during the day. Keep Jesus very close in your thoughts. As we abide and stay close to Him, He will change us to bear more of His fruit.
3. Living out the fruit of the Spirit is hard—what is natural to us are the works of the flesh in the previous verses. This fruit is not natural in our life—but by God's strength, we can get there.

Now let's take a look at these nine words that are the fruit of the Spirit and see what we can learn.

1.   Love

I think we generally get what love is—a good definition is caring for others above myself. It is kindness, yet is deeper. Love does not need to be earned—I can choose to show love to others regardless of how they respond or treat me. I think of two big ideas from God with love that I need to remember:

a)   Read **John 15:12**. God loved us first, and we now can show that love to others. The key to this idea is realizing what God's love is. In John 15, Jesus is talking about love right before He goes to the cross. That is true love—God saw us in our sinful state and loved us anyway. He considered us worth fighting for and worth buying back from Satan's hand. When Jesus was going to the cross to die for the sins of His followers, all His followers were leaving Him (**Matthew 26:56**). He died to save people who did not deserve to be saved. We have all sinned and deserve to be separate from God, and yet He freely offers us life because He loves us (**Romans 6:23**). This is love—it is undeserved. So when we think that someone does not deserve our love—we show love to that person anyway because God's love to us is underserved, and He loved us anyway.

b)   Who do we love? Read the Parable of the Good Samaritan in **Luke 10:25–37**. The parable was to a lawyer. Both he and Jesus knew what love is and how to treat others. The question was do we have to show that kind of love to everyone? The answer was a huge yes. In the parable, a Samaritan cared for a Jewish man. The Samaritans and Jews were enemies. The religious Jewish priest and Levite did not help, but the enemy and hated Samaritan did. Also, in **John 4:9**, the Samaritan woman was surprised Jesus was even talking to her. Between John 4 and Luke 10, Jesus is clearly teaching us to love everyone—even those who are very different from us. It is easy to love those who are like us; Jesus is calling us to love all humans because they are created by God. This is a message that is so needed in the world today. Followers of Jesus are called to love and care for people that are different from them: people of different races, nationalities, and backgrounds. Followers of Jesus need to be the *leaders* in understanding and caring for others who are different than them. This is the exact message of love that Jesus was sharing with the story in Luke 10.

So today, we only looked at the first fruit of the Spirit, but love is where it all begins. Again, it starts with understanding my sinfulness that has been covered by the blood of Jesus. Wow. If He loved me that much, how can I not love others? God loves others, and so should I. Stay close to God, and may He uplift you in His love.

Day 22   Galatians 5:13–26 (Part 4)

We are looking at the fruit of the Spirit in **Galatians 5:22–23,** and last time we covered the first fruit, love. Now we will look and think about what these other fruit really mean. Remember that we need to stay close to the vine (God) in order to have fruit. Feed yourself on the things of God.

2.   Joy

What is joy? It is some kind of happiness, right? But it is deep—not just being happy because my favorite movie is on—not just happy because everything went my way today, because next week might be bad. Is there a way to have joy at *all* times? Not if we are looking for happiness in this world. Whatever we gain in this life is temporary. Even if we get lots of money, money passes by—and it can't be the real answer because a lot of rich people get divorced and have law-suits—what happened to their joy? No, our joy must come from something deeper. It must come from a daily realization that the God of the universe loves me and will get me through this life somehow so that I can be with Him forever in His glory. The root of this is under-standing His love for me and accepting that love (**Romans 10:13**). Some people see who God is but never really accept Him. How sad. Remember, Jesus said whoever loses his life for His sake will find it (**Matthew 10:39**). Joy is actually hard because it is a feeling, and we can't control our feelings. But in this case, we have to choose joy by putting our minds on Jesus.

So how do I keep this in my mind? I have to remember a few truths from God. Take a look. First, **2 Corinthians 4:16–18** reminds us that whatever troubles we have now; they are temporary. If we have accepted Jesus, we have a guaranteed future with Him instead of only living for this world. This world brings a lot of pain—how wonderful to know that this is only temporary. Do not lose heart and renew your inner man each day by being focused on God.

A second passage to look at is **Hebrews 12**. In **12:1–3**, we are told to remember the suffering of Jesus—He suffered for us, and He suffered so we could have life. He is the light at the end of the tunnel, and that is good news for us, even when times are difficult. Sometimes we go through hard times because God is making something new and beautiful out of us. Hebrews **12:11** says that in hard times, we need to remember that God is at work even through pain. That pain can be turned to gain in Jesus Christ. All of that leads me to joy. Joy is knowing Him and living for Him (what really matters). Please focus on what we have in Jesus so that you can find true joy no matter what is happening around you.

3. Peace

This is a logical result of having the true joy of Jesus in you, but there are two ways of looking at the concept. One is that you are at peace and have peace in your heart. The other idea is that you are a peaceful person who is spreading peace to others you are with (a "peacemaker" and God says you are blessed—**Matthew 5:9**). So to quickly summarize "peace":

    a)   You can only have true peace when you are at peace with God. If you have been/are married, then you know that being at peace with your wife can make all else in your day good, or lack of peace with her puts a cloud over the rest of your day. It is the same with us and God. When we humbly submit to God, we have peace with Him, and it helps everything else in my life (**Romans 5:1**).

    b)   The second area of peace is peace with others. Here is the problem—people are jerks. #Facts. So it can be really hard to live in peace. But God can give us strength, and this is what God wants. **Romans 12:18** tells us to do our best in this area. The key is humility. If we always have to have the last word, then there will be no peace. We need to let the argument with that guy go. He may think we won the battle, but so what? God's peace is better. God will keep us and protect us. We do not need to fight for ourselves as much as we think we do because God sees us. Peace requires a lot of faith that God truly has me—but He truly *has* got me (**John 10:28–30**). Trust Him and live in peace with God and others.

May God encourage you in having joy and peace. He will keep you in His hand.

Day 23   Galatians 5:13–26 (Part 5)

We are still looking at the fruit of the Spirit in **Galatians 5:22–23** and have only covered three so far. Hopefully, though, we are taking time to really think about what these words mean, so the characteristics God wants us to have can grow in our lives.

4. Patience

This is a tough one. We can have patience with people who are nice, but that is easy. True patience is being kind to people who are a pain in the butt. Now, we can do this somewhat with people that we love, right? Like if you have kids, you try to be patient with them on their bad days because you love them, even though they are being pains (this sounds a little harsh, but just keeping it real). In the Bible's love chapter, it says that we show love by being patient, humble, and putting up with other people (**1 Corinthians 13:4–7**). So I can be patient with those I love, but Jesus said to love our enemies. I guess that means He wants us to be patient with everyone. Phew. Really hard, but may God give us the fruit of patience since He is a God of patience and second chances toward us.

5. and 6. Kindness and Goodness

I think we all know what it means to be kind and treat others with goodness. Remember, Jesus said to treat others how we would want to be treated ourselves. So I just want to emphasize one idea here, and that is empathy. Empathy is sympathizing and feeling what other people are feeling. Jesus understood people's needs, and thus, He empathized with them and was moved with compassion for their needs. **Matthew 14:14** shows he had compassion on the many sick people—they had physical needs, and Jesus saw that. He did something about the problem. Then there is **Matthew 9:36–38**. In these verses, Jesus is compassionate on the people because they had spiritual needs. They had no spiritual guidance in life—no shepherd. So He taught them. In summary: (a) We need to see the needs of others in order to be kind to them. Open your eyes to other people. (b) We need to be caring and compassionate people. When we see a need, do something. Be kind. Think of what they are going through, and what it would be like to be them. Be gracious and show the goodness of God with a kind heart. (c) Remember the spiritual needs of people. Sometimes, others are jerks because they have been treated terribly in life and just need Jesus.

7.   Faithfulness/Faith

Faithfulness is like faith. The ESV uses *faithfulness*, which has the idea of faith, especially when it is hard to have faith. Faithfulness is being loyal, and that is shown most when it is hard to be loyal. Almost every superhero movie has this idea of a common person in distress needing to trust someone else. He wants to trust the main character but does not understand what the hero is doing. This is when we also can get confused with the movie's plot! But then the superhero says, "Trust me," and his plan comes together. Sometimes in life, we do not know or understand what God is doing. It is at those moments we need to be faithful and trust Him.

The Bible talks about faithfulness quite a few times. In **Luke 12:35–48**, Jesus talks about a servant being ready because he does not know when the Master is returning. This is the idea of always being faithful to God and not just in good times when we see the Master (God), but even in times when we do not see God. We may not see Him, but He sees us and is still at work for us—He just asks that we be faithful when we do not understand. This was Job's issue when he was suffering. He gave his opinion of God when he was frustrated but later realized he did not know what he was talking about—Job needed to simply be faithful (**Job 40:1–5** and **42:1–3**). Job did not understand God's purposes in his suffering but had to trust that God was at work—and He was. Job did realize this at times since he also said, "Naked I came from my mother's womb, and naked shall I return. The Lord gave, and the Lord has taken away; blessed be the name of the Lord" (**Job 1:21–22**). That is trust and faithfulness in times of confusion.

My point in all of this is that often, we do not understand what is happening to us in life. These are the times we just have to be faithful to God and trust. Anyone can be faithful to God in good times; God asks us to trust Him in hard times. He is at work even when we don't see it. May God give you strength to be faithful at all times.

Day 24   Galatians 5:13–26 (Part 6)

God's fruit of the spirit is God's word lived out. When we pray for ourselves to grow in God, these are the specific areas we are praying for in our lives. Today, the last two fruits:

8.   Gentleness

What do you think are the qualities of a real man? Strength and leadership, I am sure come to mind. What about gentleness? It is not exactly a quality we aspire to. We rarely say, "I hope I can be more gentle." Yet gentleness is one of the fruits of the spirit. Not only that, Jesus showed gentleness to many people, which helped draw them to Him. Two incidents come to mind: In **Mark 10:13–16**, the disciples chased kids away, but Jesus accepted them and told his disciples they should be more like kids. These children felt safe with Jesus. See, gentleness leads to leadership because people want to follow you or be around you. Jesus was also gentle to a blind man in **Mark 10:46–52**. Again, others did not care for this blind beggar and told him to shut up, while Jesus cared for him and healed him.

We need to value gentleness because gentleness values people. People who are poor, shy, and fearful feel safe around someone who is gentle. My being gentle with people shows that I love those people and care for their feelings. We want to be treated gently, so why wouldn't we treat others with gentleness? As we see God gently accepting us, we understand gentleness more.

9.   Self-control

This is a big one. How are you doing with self-control? If you are like me, you would say that you have great self-control as long as people aren't being idiots. Of course, that is when we need self-control the most. Actually, there are two areas in which we really need self-control in our life:

- Self-control to stay away from things that are bad for us. These could be addictions or could be negative responses we have (like we get angry too quickly). At that moment, we have to look to Jesus so we can avoid falling again. Jesus is the key to our self-control. Remember, He can give us the strength to NOT sin, but we do need to focus on Him and stay close to Him for this to happen. Read **1 Corinthians 10:13**.

- Self-control to do hard things that make us better in the end. Sometimes, my kids have a hard time getting out of bed in the morning. It is easy and fun for them to sleep in all day. But they would miss school, and even though they would be happy about that today, eventually they would be eighteen years old and still in first grade. It is better to get out of bed and go to school! In the same way, we need self-control to stay close to God. For example, it is interesting how hard it is to pray—so simple and yet hard to focus and actually do. We need self-control to do what is not always easy in order to move ahead in life and with our walk with God. Reading the Bible slowly, meditating on it, and praying are so easy…and so hard. We need self-control to do the things we need to stay close to Him.

Wow. Those are impressive characteristics—all nine of them. Stay close to God and grow in His fruit. BUT **Galatians 5:24** reminds us that we do not naturally follow God's fruit. Our natural passions and desires are against God, and this verse tells us to crucify those desires. That is pretty serious—crucify—like really put to death each day our own natural sinful desires so that we can advance closer to God. I know whom I cannot trust the most. I see him in the mirror each morning. It is the same with you—you cannot trust yourself and your desires. They will lead you down a wrong path, and some-day you will say how did I get here? Your desires! So the answer to that situation is a daily killing of my natural, sinful desires (they won't help me anyway) and a daily recommitment to God. Jesus said this in **Luke 9:23**.

In some ways, the real question is how serious are we about changing? Part of us really wants to change and become more like Jesus—part of us likes our old desires. After all, it was fun for a while. We have got to see Jesus for who He is—the God who loves us and knows what is best for us. Stay close to Him, renew each day, and grow in the fruit of the Spirit. May God guide us all in this. Next time, we still have two more verses to look at here in Galatians 5. May God give strength.

Day 25   Galatians 5:13–26 (Part 7)

This is the last day we will spend on this passage of Scripture, but we need to see the conclusion. These verses have been all about real life, challenging us to live according to God and not following our own fleshly desires. The conclusion is in **Galatians 5:25–26**. Verse 25 is the summary statement, and verse 26 is the warning.

A. Verse 25—Live life by the Spirit

It starts by saying, "If we live by the Spirit." This phrase is reminding us how we got life. Do you have a life with God for eternity ahead of you? If so, how did you get that? Was it because of your good works? Was it because you were born a "Christian"? No! The only way to get life is by accepting Jesus and what He did for us— that is not a good work we do; it is our spirit, our heart, being humble and saying, "I need God." This is a spiritual acceptance because we could never work our way to God anyway (**Ephesians 2:8–9**). So verse 25 tells us, since we received life from God, we should "walk" or "keep in step" (live out this life) according to God also. Why would we claim to be on God's team and then not live that way? What does it look like to live according to God's way? He just told us—it looks like the fruit of the Spirit in the previous verses.

Overall, God is just telling us not to be hypocrites. We received life by God, now live by God. Embrace His Spirit, and may our life match what we say. Now, if you are not in Christ—if you are not sure you have life in the spirit—then you need to start there. Stop trusting in your own works and accept Jesus's work that he did for us on the cross (**Romans 5:8, 6:23,** and **10:9, 13**). We will never achieve a life that looks like the fruit of the Spirit until we accept Him first. He did all the work for us and wants us.

B. Verse 26—Warning: Watch out for yourself

This verse first tells us not to be conceited. That is the idea that I am something special. It is me saying that I am living a good life, and it is all because of me. It is saying, "I got this." This is very dangerous. You know those epic fail videos on YouTube? Probably, the last words the guy said before failing were "I got this." Imagine if we started following the fruit of the spirit and were showing love and gentleness. Then we started thinking how much better we were than others because we are more kind than them. This would be our undoing—this would cause us to fail. We cannot ever think that we have "got this" because of us. It all needs to come back to Jesus, every single day.

Notice it says in verse 26 that when we become conceited and full of ourselves, we provoke one another. Basically, when we become full of ourselves, we become jerks, and other people can't stand to be around us. How true is that? One of our biggest dangers in walking the Christian life is thinking we are better than others because we are walking the Christian life. This pride is nothing but harmful sin.

There is a third phrase in verse 26 also—"envying one another." Envy is another version of pride. Envy is looking at someone else and saying why didn't I get that chance? Why did he get to do that? What about me? Ultimately, it is desiring that I be taken care of before anyone else—I want mine. Envy is a way of saying I don't think God is treating me fairly because I don't have what that person has. Okay, deep breath. We have to trust that God knows what He is doing and that He has got us. We have to rest in Him and grow in the fruit of the Spirit—no matter what. Don't get distracted by what other people are doing and getting. Pride is the enemy of spiritual growth and personal growth. Every day we have to look to God and not to ourselves.

These verses in Galatians can be life-changing if we remember them and seek to live by them. This takes a daily reminding of who God is, what we have in Jesus, and focus on areas we need to work on. Look again at these verses and choose two of the fruits of the Spirit to really work on this week. May God give you strength in growing in His fruit and becoming more like Him.

Day 26 God's Righteousness Romans 3:21–26

This is important. What is the Bible, God's message to all mankind, really all about? This passage of **Romans 3:21–26** gives us the core of all Bible teaching in just a few verses. It is important for us to understand what is written here so that we see what the main message of the Bible is. Take a few minutes to read these verses through two or three times.

"God's righteousness." Maybe we could call this "God's holiness" or "the essence of who He really is." Now, how do we see that? Verses 21–22 tell us that God's righteousness is shown and available through Jesus Christ. Notice that God's righteousness is not found through keeping the Law, but through "faith in Jesus Christ for all who believe." So these verses are about how we can achieve God's righteousness, and it is clearly not through works but by surrendering to God by accepting Jesus. This is important because verse 23 reminds us who is worthy of God's righteousness—no one! We all fall short!

Now we need to see how this affects all of us because, let's face it, we like to compare ourselves to others. We can always find people who are worse than us (or so we think), and then we think that we are doing okay because we are better than that guy. We even excuse our sins by saying, "Well, I didn't really *mean* to do that." Romans 3:23 tells us that no matter who we are, myself included, we all fall short of God and who He is. This is a problem for me. Good thing, God loves me enough to make a way for me to join Him in His righteousness that does not depend on me. Read verse 24.

God wants us to join His goodness. He wants us to join HIM so we can be "justified" (we are looked upon "just as if" we never sinned) "by His grace as a gift." Wow. A gift! Imagine receiving a package, and inside is eternal life through Jesus! And in the meantime, God's Spirit to guide us through life right now! That is quite a gift. And I did not even earn it because that is the definition of gift—something I can receive for no reason since I do not deserve it. This gift is possible because of "the redemption that is in Christ Jesus." Redemption means to buy back. I sold myself to sin. I thought life without God was going to be so fun—and it was for a while, but then it landed me in worse position than before. And I am ashamed before a holy God. And then this holy God pays the penalty for my sin to buy me back from the power of sin and bring me to Him. Wow! I am redeemed!

Verses 25–26 explain the process. This word *propitiation* means in my place, God made the payment. It was Jesus's blood that was shed for my sin and not my blood. Now why did Jesus have to pay for my sin? It says part of the reason is to **show** God's righteousness. Show. God wanted us to really see and understand how much He wants us on His team, so He did not merely say He loved us. He showed it. He did the work and offers it to us by faith. Faith—an accepting of who He is. Faith is saying yes to God. All of this allows God to be "just and the justifier" of us. This important phrase shows that God is still holy. He is the definition of goodness. He does not simply excuse our sin by saying, "Awww, that is okay." No, our sin makes this world a broken place. Sin is serious. God's stand against sin makes Him "just." But He knows we all go toward sin in our lives, so He also provided the answer for our sin: Jesus. This makes Him the "justifier" of our lives. What do we need to do? Have "faith in Jesus." That is accepting Him—telling Him you want to be on His team. It is that deep, and yet it is that simple.

This is what the Bible is all about. This is what we call the gospel. It is important for us who know the gospel to remember it every day. We need to remember who God is and how He then provided us with the answer in Jesus. This keeps us humble and grateful. We need to be able to share this gospel message with people around us. We need to explain it clearly and be able to show verses like Romans 3 so people understand. But if you haven't made that decision to join God's team, you need to make a choice of what you will do with Jesus and the gift He is offering. Way too many people say, "I'm all right," when they are not all right. We are not all right before God. Look at the broken world we live in. Too many people have ignored God in their lives. If you have also, it is time to tell God you want Jesus. He paid it all for us. May we all keep thinking about these important verses—memorize them so you always have the gospel message with you.

Day 27   Lessons from David (Part 1)

Over the coming days, I would like to look at a few incidents from the life of David and see what we can learn from them. God called David "a man after his own heart." That is quite a statement, and we see that while David was not perfect, he definitely had some qualities that are worth following. Today we will start with seeing what actually matters—our heart; this is our character and integrity.

The first time we meet David is when he is chosen from among his brothers to be the future king of Israel. So, to begin, read **1 Samuel 16:1–13**. In this passage, we see the prophet Samuel going to the house of Jesse to anoint the next king while the current king is still alive and well! Since this is kind of a dangerous thing to do, Samuel also does some sacrifices so he can say he was there for religious reasons. Now, Samuel sees these sons of Jesse and starts with the oldest, Eliab. He is a handsome guy and a tall, strong guy. Samuel is impressed. Maybe Eliab had been working out for the previous months and was pretty ripped at the time. Samuel thinks he would make a great leader, BUT God steps in and says *no* in verse 7. This verse 7 is the key because God says that He does not look at people's outward appearance, but He looks at the heart. Later, insignificant David is chosen, who ironically is still described as handsome, but we now know he also has a heart that is sensitive to God. David was so insignificant in this family, by the way, that he did not get the invitation to meet the famous prophet but was still out in the field watching sheep.

What do you think is the big lesson here? Our heart, the inside, is most important, right? Our world today is pretty obsessed with the outward appearance. A lot of social media is based on showing off your looks. God says something totally different. **1 Timothy 4:6–8** shows us what is really most important. These verses tell us that bodily exercise does have some benefit—that is true. But too often, we leave out of our life the training in godliness. Training to become more like Jesus is so much more important than physical training. It is also a lot harder—why? (1) It is abstract. How do we measure our godliness? That is not easy to do. (2) Godliness needs to be renewed each day. We cannot say "I worked extra hard yesterday on godliness, so screw everyone else today." (Can I print that, by the way, as a chaplain? I guess I just did). No, yesterday's godly attitudes need to be renewed today. This very daily refocusing is hard to do. (3) It is hard to be godly in this ungodly world. If I am being godly, I will need to show self-control instead of self-indulgence. If I am being godly, I will not be able to get revenge on someone; I will need to forgive. That forgiveness is not easy to get caught up in, and yet that is how I grow in godliness and character. I forgive like Jesus did, and I love like Jesus loves me. That is true character and having the heart of God.

Jesus actually reserved His harshest criticism in this area for those who claimed to be following God but were only concerned about their outside good appearance and not their hearts. In **Matthew 23:25–28**, Jesus calls out the Pharisees for looking good on the outside but giving in to self-indulgence on the inside. They were selfish and did not truly care about loving others—only that others loved them and respected them. They had no humility and only hypocrisy. Read **Matthew 15:10–11, 18–20**. Here, Jesus shows that our heart is most important. It is from the selfishness of our heart that evil things come. Character matters, not outward appearance.

So back to David; even godly Samuel was fooled into thinking Eliab was a good choice for king because of his appearance. Remember that God looks on the heart. This can be encouraging to us or discouraging. If you are focused on pushing people around to get your way, this is discouraging. If you are focused on showing how good you are, this is discouraging. If you are focused on serving God and getting closer to God and not a lot of people have noticed this, then this is encouraging. God sees our hearts.

Take time to develop your heart each day. Spend time with God, read His word, think about it, and always consider God when thinking about your life. Consider God when thinking of others also, so you can treat others like Jesus does. This is not easy, and I know I do not always have a heart fully devoted to God, but that is our goal: that God can look at our heart and see us moving closer to Him each day. We will see specific examples of David's heart in the coming days.

Day 28　　　　Lessons from David (Part 2)

Today, let's get to the most famous part of David's story. We all have heard of David and Goliath. I want us to see how it truly went down, so read **I Samuel 17**. This entire chapter is the David and Goliath story. What stands out to you from it? Are there some lessons you think apply to us today?

Well, traditionally this story gets told in Sunday school to little kids, and the lesson for them is that God will always help you conquer the giants in your life. Then we go out into life and get defeated by some giants—some literally and some figuratively—and we wonder where God was. So let's be sure we are learning correctly from the story. It is a true story here in the history section of the Bible. It is also very believable because the slingshot people back then were very accurate, and those stones flying through the air would kill you if you got hit in the head. That does not mean God wasn't with David—He clearly was. It took a great amount of courage for David to take on Goliath (who was around nine feet tall, seemingly from a family with genetic issues, whose descendants died out)—so why did David do this and no one else? That is a very big question—take a look at what lessons are here for us, starting with one that is not.

Lesson that is not—This chapter is telling us what David did and how God worked for him. It does not mean that God will work this way every time for everybody. God saw the big picture and knew this victory was best for David at this time. Do not go around punching people bigger than you, thinking that you will be like David and God will help you beat up giants today. Besides, we know that if we want to live a godly life, we will suffer (**2 Timothy 3:12**), so let's not think that since David won, we will then defeat every problem in our life—we can have victories, but life is also full of problems.

Lesson 1—God can help. Even though I just said this does not mean we will never have problems; it does show us that God can help us. In the big picture, we KNOW that if things are not working out like we want, that we can trust Him because He is shaping us, even through difficulty, to be more like Jesus (**Romans 8:28–29**). David had victory and fully trusted that God would work His will. God chose to work through victory this day, but another day He might choose to work through problems. This is faith, and we can trust the outcome no matter what it may be because God is trustworthy (**Proverbs 3:5–6**).

Lesson 2—God's honor is worth it. Now this, I believe, is the main lesson of the story. David came to the battle scene and was upset. Why? Because here was this guy insulting Israel's God and saying that their God could not help them against him. Whoa. David took a stand for what is right. But wait—David had to take a stand among God's own people too—among his own family! David's brother was questioning David's motives and was still jealous over David being chosen by Samuel to be future king. David had to stand up to him and do what was right, no matter what. Why? Because the cause of God is worth it.

Hey, not everyone in your life will be excited for you if you give your life fully to God. You might not get encouragement from your family to walk in the path of God—David didn't. This is reality, but David knew he had God, and that was enough. This fact is hard to follow through with in real life—to stand for God and really live a new life among those who knew you before. Many of your "friends" may leave you since you don't hang out with them anymore and don't do what they do anymore. Take courage. Jesus said God will provide more people for you in your life to care for you when you are left alone for His name's sake. Read **Mark 10:28–30**. God is with us no matter what the outcome.

Do you have some giants in your life? Are there some situations that are really hard for you? I can't say that this story means they will work out exactly like you want. I can say that God will be with you when life gets difficult and you feel alone. God is there and sees you. He will give you victory too—it just might not be exactly a victory like you think. But that is okay. He loves you and is trustworthy to be shaping you into someone that trusts Him more. God is worth it. God is worth your life.

Day 29   Lessons from David (Part 3)

Today we will cover one of the biggest lessons that David learned early in his life, which is one of the hardest lessons we need to learn for our lives. The lesson is to let God take care of other people. Do you have people in your life that drive you crazy? Do you know people who did you wrong? Are there people out there that you need to get even with because of how they treated you? I think we all have those kinds of people in our lives, so let's see how this lesson looked in David's life and what it means for us today. Start by reading **1 Samuel chapter 24**. Take a moment to review what happened and then read on.

Saul was trying to kill David because of his own selfishness and jealousy. David was running for his life and in this chapter has a chance to take care of the problem. Instead, he spares Saul's life. Make sure you see how justified David would have been in killing Saul—David had not broken the law. Saul was not living for God. David's men told him that God gave him this chance to make things right. David could clearly get away with killing Saul here—and yet he didn't. In verse 7, we see David even had to persuade his men to calm down and not kill Saul. David could have taken care of his Saul problem at this time but instead chose to put the whole situation into God's hand. Not only that, but he had another chance to get Saul in **1 Samuel 26**, but David spared his life again. So what lessons are here for us?

This is really tough, but we have to learn to let God be the judge of people, not us. Look at **1 Samuel 24:12**. David said God would judge who is right, but that wasn't David's job, and he would not lift his hand against Saul. Wow. That is trust. That takes an immense amount of *self-control*. We definitely want to take care of other people ourselves and be done with them. David turned Saul over to God. I had a big moment in my life where I was struggling with some people in authority, and I thought I was right. But that was a time where I had to learn to let God handle the situation rather than getting in there and forcing my will on everyone. That was hard. Sometimes it looks like weakness. I am sure David's men thought he was wimping out and not being a man, but this was a huge step of faith—faith that God will take care of that person. Can you do that? Can you let God take care of the problem people in your life? I know that was a hard lesson for me.

Notice something else though—at the end of the chapter, Saul apologizes for chasing David. Did David accept that apology? Yes. Did David then trust Saul? No. Verse 22 says that David went back to his stronghold and did not go with Saul back to the city. Forgiveness and trust are not the same thing. I can forgive, and I can turn someone over to God, but that still might mean that I walk away from that relationship right now. It might not be a good time to be together. I need to trust that God will take care of that person and keep my distance. That is what David did here. He wisely did not fully trust Saul, even though he let him go. That is the faith of letting go and letting God take care of your situation. David was a man of peace in this situation and knew that being near Saul was not good for him at this time. So David put Saul in God's hand and walked away.

What does this mean for you? I do not know your situation now. This lesson might not apply to every situation in your life. I do know that there came a time in my life where I could choose to really fight out a situation, or I could just walk away. Sometimes God does want us to stay and fight for a cause, but in my situation, I saw these verses and knew that I needed to walk away and let God do what He needed to do in the lives of those other people. Letting God handle situations is hard because we want to DO something, and sometimes, we really want to fight for ourselves. David let God fight for him. David walked away, and it was for the best. God did protect David. God did punish Saul, and David was rewarded in becoming king later on. It was all in God's timing. We do not see the whole picture—trust God's timing. Take a deep breath and wait on the Lord. As this chapter shows us, sometimes the hardest thing to do is to do nothing but trust God. Trust Him to handle your life. He is trustworthy.

Day 30   Lessons from David (Part 4)

Today is a story from David's life that is not very common. I find it an interesting incident in David's life with a few lessons for us to learn. First, we need to read **1 Samuel chapter 25**. Try to read it and summarize it to yourself, and then I will talk about it in the next paragraph before we get to the lessons.

Basically, David helped the servants of this rich idiot named Nabal—even his wife says that he is stupid (verse 25). When David asks for a little help from Nabal because of the protection he gave his men, Nabal refuses and insults David's men. David gets angry and is ready to attack Nabal (and probably kill him) when Nabal's wife, Abigail, comes to protect undeserving Nabal and pay David for his service. David is humbled by this noble act and repents of his temper (verse 33). Later, when Nabal finds out what happened and how he was almost killed, he has a heart attack and dies. In the end, David marries Abigail. Hmmm, what lessons can we learn?

1. Don't be Nabal! He did not want to be kind to David's men, nor did he listen to other people (verse 17). That is big. Listen to others. This could have been solved if Nabal just listened to his servants, but the servants said Nabal does not listen—he is so worthless that "one cannot speak to him." Wow. We need to be kind enough to talk to people and be willing to listen. Read **James 1:19**.

2. David lost his temper. Don't! In our last lesson we saw that David was incredibly patient and peaceful. He did not kill Saul when he had the chance and let God handle the situation. We said yesterday that that is a very hard lesson—to let God handle our issues and problem people in our life. It is so hard a lesson that David himself forgot it here. In the end, David confessed in verse 33 that he was taking matters into his own hand instead of trusting God to work it out. So we are reminded here again of the importance of letting

God handle difficult people in our life. Do not seek revenge or solve the problem of another person your way. Let God handle that person, even if you know he is in the wrong and you are right. David learned that here and confessed that he was going to kill Nabal—and Abigail saved David from not trusting God. Let God work. In this story, God did punish Nabal—that might not happen every time, but we can be the bigger man by letting God handle our issues.

3. Do what is right even if others don't deserve it. This was Abigail. She went and stood in the way so that her loser husband was protected. This was a big deal since he did not deserve her protection, and even she admitted he was an idiot. Yet for the sake of the servants, she went and protected Nabal. We may be in situations where we have a job with an idiot boss or have to deal with terrible teammates. We still need to stand for what is right and do what is right. Abigail was clearly ready to get out of this marriage, but she was still going to stand for what was right, even if it benefitted Nabal.

4. One man, one woman! Now, at the end of the chapter Nabal is judged. That is great that God gave him what he deserved here on earth—that is not guaranteed. But it did not mean David was supposed to marry Abigail when he already had another wife. This happened a lot in the culture back then, especially among kings, but we do not see God blessing this act. We do not receive any comment here about whether it was good or bad that David had multiple wives, but later in his life, we see David's family had nothing but trouble because there were so many different mothers of David's kids. One man, one woman.

Overall, we see both today and last time that we tend to try to take care of problem people ourselves. No. We have got to give problem people to God and let Him handle them. David succeeded in giving Saul over to God, but he almost failed in giving Nabal over to God. Don't make yourself the judge of all other people. Trust God and let Him work. This is one of the only times we see David losing his temper like this, and he admits he was wrong. Pray for difficult people rather than attacking them. I am praying for you that you may grow in God and remember Him each day, especially when you get out of here. God bless.

Day 31   Lessons from David (Part 5)

Worship. Sometimes we men think of that as a weak word—worship is for women or for men who are into emotional stuff too much. The problem with that thinking is David was really big on worship, and he was also a fighter warrior. He had a life balanced between being a strong leader of men and a worshiper of God who was all-in with showing his love for God. No chapter shows this better than **2 Samuel 6**. David is now king, and one of his first acts is to bring the ark of the covenant home. This goes bad at first because God is holy, and Uzzah disobeyed God's rules, but later the journey is completed, and David lets himself go in worship. Read that chapter now, and we will see a few lessons about worship from it.

The key moment in the chapter is David dancing before the ark. He does not wear his royal robes as befitting a king, and his first wife Michal resents him for it. She says the servant girls saw him without his royal clothes, and that is beneath him as king. He responds saying he doesn't care because the people know he is worshipping God—so Michal can think what she wants, but he will be held in honor before those that truly love God. Phew! Big words. Arguing. And Michal is judged, so we know David is right in his worship. What lessons can we take out of that cultural context and apply to us today? Here is what I think:

1. Worship is from the heart. David's active worship was because his heart was overflowing with love for God and the representation of that in bringing the ark home. David was sincere and joyful. Sometimes we as people worship God in different ways—active songs, quiet songs, a quiet walk or meditation, group prayer, prayer alone. All of these ways of worship are fine because God sees our heart.
2. God deserves our best. David shouted with all his might and danced before God. He sacrificed to God that day.

Why? God deserves our whole heart and all of our efforts. He deserves our best.

3. In a community of Jesus followers, we are all equal. We can all worship together because we are on equal standing before God—none of us deserves Him, and yet God loves us anyway. There was no difference in David's eyes between him and the servant girls. Michal thought differently, but David realized he was worshipping God, and before God, he was no better than anyone else.

4. Worship is joyful. When we understand who we are (sinners) and who God is (holy) and what God did for us (saved us by His grace **Ephesians 2:8–9, Romans 5:6–9**), we should be filled with humility, gratefulness, and joyfulness that we get to be on God's team. He loves us even though we fail Him. Wow! That is something worth being joyful about. He deserves our worship.

5. God is still holy. At this point in history, God was still showing His people who He was, and they needed to understand He is very holy. This is why Uzzah was judged harshly for not following God's rules. It is a reminder of what we deserve because we are not holy, and how gracious God actually is with us.

6. It is not about us. Michal was concerned how she and David would look in this worship time. What would the people think? David did not care because it was not about him—it was about God. He was willing to worship God from his heart no matter what. He focused on God and not his own human position.

Where does all this leave us? Worship God. Find some ways that help you really connect with God in your heart. I like listening to worship music—it sets my heart on God's joy. I also like taking walks and listening to sermons. It focuses me on God's word. I know some people spend a lot of time in quiet prayer, praising God and praying through prayers like those in the Psalms. Some people write their thoughts down and praise God through a journal. It does not matter how you connect with God—but take time to connect with God. You can worship God wherever you are (Daniel did—he prayed daily when he was in captivity). The key is finding ways that lighten your heart and put your focus on God and all He has done in saving us, while also looking forward to an eternity with Him. Don't worry about what other people will think when you tell them you are spending some time getting your worship on! Maybe they will see your joy and even join you. Hey, if you can have joy during these days in this place, then that is something to praise God about! But He truly wants to give you joy and knows you can find it in Him. Remember, it is all about Him.

Have a worshipful day.

Day 32   Lessons from David (Part 6)

Today we will see a couple small lessons (although every lesson has big implications for our lives) from the life of David. First, read **2 Samuel 7:12–22**. This is part of a chapter where God promises to work through David's descendants forever (showing us Jesus will come from David's line and will forever be at work), and David praises God for His blessings. What do you think we can learn from this?

I feel like verse 18 is one of the most beautiful verses in the Bible, and it shows an amazing amount of humility from a guy who has defeated all his enemies at this point in his life. David killed Goliath and defeated others; he was the king now—and yet he says, "Who am I?" That is a question that shows humility. We really need humility these days. So many guys in the world today just want to be The Man and make sure everyone else knows that. Yet this response from David shows that he understood life is all about God and not about us.

Humility—it is an attitude that realizes I am special only because of God and not because of myself. Pride gets me in trouble. Pride makes me run over other people instead of valuing other people. Take a look at these verses: **Philippians 2:3–5**. These are huge verses when it comes to humility lived out. Pride boosts concern for myself because I need to make sure no one else is above me. I am so concerned with myself that I am blind to the needs of others, and I do not help others. We will see this humility in David momentarily. Because he saw himself in the right way, he was ready and available to reach out and help others.

That brings us to the next story in David's life that we will look at found in **2 Samuel 9**. Read the chapter and think about that story. David is showing great kindness to this guy, Mephibosheth (say that name fast five times!) simply because of who he was. Since he was a son of David's friend Jonathan (Saul's son), David reached out to him and brought him close. It is interesting because that is what God does with us—God does not love us because of what we do for Him or if we are earning His favor. He loves us because we are His creation, and we become a child of God because of Him. We have this amazing position all because He saw us, still sees us, and loves us. That is the picture of what David is doing with Mephibosheth.

Also, notice how Mephibosheth is really defined by his disability. In verse 3, the first thing said about him is that he is a son of Jonathan but is crippled. Then in verse 8, Mephibosheth seems a little over the top calling himself a "dead dog." Again, he has probably felt pretty worthless through his whole life and can't believe that the king is calling him. Then by the time we get to verse 11, we see he is treated like one of David's own sons. Wow. So look at this story through your own eyes. You may have had moments where you felt worthless and not seen. I think we all have those times. Yet we have to trust and know that God sees us. There is hope for the future, and that hope is not based on ourselves or what we have to accomplish, but our hope is based on God, our Father, who wants to take us from where we are and make us His children. It is a big deal. This truth was for Mephibosheth, and it is for us. Okay, to summarize, here are a few lessons we saw:

- I deserve nothing. God gives me everything. Wow! And by everything, we mean that which really matters for eternity, not just stuff to use right now.
- I need a proper view of myself so that in humility I can reach out to others.
- Don't let a label keep you from God. He can carry you. We get this from Mephibosheth, the cripple, who became someone important and valued despite a label.
- Look for those you can reach out to and help. David was sitting in a position of strength and wanted to share that with others. This is how Mephibosheth was called. When we are blessed, look to share that blessing with others, especially those who are different from us.

These are just a few small thoughts today, but these lessons are not insignificant to the ones you reach out to and help. Have a humble heart like David.

Day 33   Lessons from David (Part 7)

2 Samuel 11. Here we are. This is the famous story of David's sin with Bathsheba. It is a big warning about how any of us is capable of any sin—we have to be on the guard against sin in our lives. To help us out, let's see the steps of David's sin so we can avoid them in our lives. Read the chapter, think about how this happened, and notice the last words of the chapter.

Let's look at the steps to sin by David. Before I start the list, notice verse 1. Was David supposed to be at battle? Maybe, so he might have not been in the right place at the right time because of his own choice not to go. Was David relaxing and not busy? Yes. Was David alone without many others to check on him? Yes. Look, before we leave verse 1, we already see problems. We need to be doing what we are supposed to—David might not have been. David was definitely relaxed, which is when we let our guard down. We don't usually sin when we are busy at work; it is the party after work that is the problem. Then David was alone—we need to be accountable to others. We need people in our life that will ask us tough questions about ourselves and will check in on us. David sent all those people away. No one will know what he is up to. This is a recipe for disaster.

1. Verse 2. David looked...and kept looking. With his free time, he looked around and saw this woman. Don't blame her. The king's house was probably the only house that could see her, and the king was supposed to be out fighting with his men. Now, sometimes we see things we shouldn't or are suddenly somewhere that we shouldn't be—that might not be our fault. But the second look is our fault. David did not look and look away. He looked and kept looking. Trouble.
2. Verse 3. David thought about it. He asked about her. He kept playing with her in his mind. We cannot give sin this foothold. We must get away from the bad situation. We

must pray. We might even just need to go for a walk in the other direction. Some of this battle is spiritual, but some is practical. Get away. Do something else and get your mind away from the sinful situation.

3. Verse 4. He called her. Now he is choosing to get close to sin instead of running from sin. After that, he commits the act. Perhaps he thought she would not get pregnant, and he would get away with it. Doesn't matter. It was all wrong and all sin. It was giving in to a momentary pleasure without considering the long-term impact on a life. We do this type of reasoning in our heads all the time. We have to remember God and remember our long-term goals of life, not just living for the moment.

4. The cover-up. So David sinned. He sinned against Bathsheba because she had to obey the king. He sinned against Uriah, Bathsheba's husband, because he stole from him. He sinned against his own family by not being faithful. Most of all, David sinned against God. So he tried to cover it up. He tried to get Uriah to sleep with his wife, so the baby would be thought of as his, but he was too noble and committed to his army job. In the end, David made sure Uriah died so David could take Bathsheba. 2 Samuel 11:27 shows that God was not happy. David sinned against God.

There are so many problems here, but I want to emphasize two major lessons: (a) David's sin began well before he slept with the woman. He could have fought this sin right away by walking away, but he stayed, he lingered, he played out the "good times" in his mind. We have to fight sin early and quickly. Stop your mind from going down that path because once you start in that direction, it is way harder to stop from sinning. (b) Do not sacrifice your future for a moment of pleasure. Sin, any sin, gives us temporary benefit or pleasure. That is why we sin—that is why we lie, cheat, etc. But too often, we fail to think about the deep consequences. Basically, David's longing look after a woman turned into murder. Yes, that escalated very quickly. But that is what sin does, and we have to cover it up and go deeper and deeper down the hole that we are digging for ourselves. At some point, we say, "How did I get here?" and the answer is usually a small decision that went out of control. Stop sin early. Do not sacrifice your future for a moment of sin today.

We all sin. Is there any hope for us now? Yes. Tomorrow we will see.

Day 34   Lessons from David (Part 8)

Yesterday we saw David's sin. David's actions in 2 Samuel 11 are a big warning to us. I mean, think about it, David was such a good king—he was sympathetic and caring to other people. He always cared about those who were hurting and even refused to kill King Saul, who had been chasing him, when he had the chance. And yet he was willing to kill Uriah, this faithful man, so that he could get Uriah's wife for himself. I don't think David woke up and said today I am going to steal another man's wife, but once he saw Bathsheba, David let his mind go and gave in to his own desires; one thing led to another in the cover-up, and next thing you know, David has cheated another man out of his wife and killed him for it. I don't think we wake up one day and say, "Today I want to ruin my life," but sometimes we do make decisions that really hurt us and others. That is what sin does. I think the Bible includes this story of David to show that it can happen to anyone, so we better wake up each day and commit ourselves to God because a little thing can become a big thing really fast. Control temptation while it is small. God says we can do this in **1 Corinthians 10:13**. God will provide a way to escape the temptation and not sin. The problem is that we linger and hang around sin until it is too late. At that point, we have already given in to our sinful desires, and we are left with the consequences. We looked at **Galatians 5:16–17** not too long ago, and we need to remember that our natural desires are not in line with God.

At the end of 2 Samuel 11, we see the child born—David hid his sin for at least nine months, but God knew. So He sent the prophet Nathan along to tell David a story. Read **2 Samuel 12:1–14**. The sheep story shows what David really did. It wasn't just a small love affair—it was much bigger. David himself was outraged at the guy who stole the one little sheep from the poor man in the story, and Nathan dramatically declared that David was that man. David did not consider the cost of his sin on others. We rarely do. We are just following our passions. The world says we are following our heart, but that is not always a good thing to do. The good part of this story is that David repents and gets forgiveness. Read verses 15–23 for the conclusion. The baby does die, but David knows that is also his fault and worships God at the end of the story. David is forgiven but still heavy with the results of his sin.

This is a hard story and sad story. But it is real, and there is hope. When verse 23 ends, it is over. David is good with God again and can regain that relationship with Him (more on that next time). This actually is one of the reasons David is called a man after God's own heart. The king before him, Saul, sinned and made excuses for that sin (read **1 Samuel 13:8–14** and **1 Samuel 15:10–30**. In 15:21, Saul blames other people for his sin, and in 15:30, Saul is still concerned with his own honor even when he admitted he sinned), but David admitted his sin when confronted. He made no excuses. He truly repented. God knows that we are not perfect, but do we know that? Sometimes we walk around like everyone else in the world has sin problems, but not us, since we are right all the time. We are never wrong. David was not like this—he realized he was a sinner who had been made king. We saw that he was humble about this fact just a couple chapters ago. Since his heart was humble, he could get right with God again.

I want to take one more day to look at David's repentant heart. Later today, you can also read **Psalm 51**, and we will study it tomorrow. It is the psalm David wrote at this time to express his sorrow over his sin and desire to be right with God again. It is so important because every one of us is a sinner. I need that humble heart, like we all do. But from today, let us remember the lessons of being quick to take responsibility for our own actions. David made no excuses. Let's also be quick to say I am sorry. We need to say that to God and other people. It is not a sign of weakness to apologize; it is actually a sign of strength. God accepts apologies and wants us back. God wanted David back, which is why He sent the prophet to him. God wants you. He is ready for you. If you are far from him, turn back. God is always ready to take us back.

Day 35   Lessons from David (Part 9)

The last few days, we looked at David's big sin. Today, we see the rebuilding of David—this is how He got right with God and was able to move forward. It is found in his prayer, which is **Psalm 51**. Take some time to read this psalm slowly, looking at David's heart being shown through his words. He realized how his sin had broken his relationship with God. What stands out to you in the psalm? I am going to comment on verses that stand out to me. There are many—and this will take two days—but it is just that important because we all sin, and we all need to get back to God at various times in our life.

Verse 1. Notice that David is calling on God's mercy based on His "steadfast love" and "abundant mercy." This is all we've got. We cannot say, "Forgive me because I am a great person. Look at all I did for you." No, how could we say that to God? We have nothing but His love and mercy to fall on. The good news is God is okay with this and wants us so much that He is ready to show His mercy. **Romans 3:23–26**.

Verse 2. David says, "Wash me thoroughly…" This is a complete cleaning because sin can dominate our lives. Just like in David's sin, something starts off pretty small but then becomes really big in our lives. It is like we need a complete cleaning to rid our lives of the sin. David realizes he does not need a little bit of cleaning, but complete cleaning. Some people try to hold on to a little bit of their life of sin. They say, "I am doing better than I was before." While that is progress, we can use that as an excuse to keep hanging on to a little bit more of our sin. We need to be completely cleansed from our sin.

Verse 3. David admitted here that he knew his sin. Let's not play games with God. He knows us. He knows our thoughts. We need to own up to our sin before God. When Jesus was around, there were people who thought they were pretty good, so Jesus called them (and us) out. In **Matthew 5:27–28**, Jesus says that sin happens in our heart long before an act is committed. God sees our lustful heart or our angry heart (**Matthew 5:21–22**) and calls it for what it is—sin.

David in verse 3 said his sin was ever before him. Yes, David had to stop hiding his sin and pretending. He admitted to God his sin.

Verse 4. David realized that his sin was against God. God loves every person. David did not treat other people the right way. He took advantage of his earthly power to steal a man's wife and then get rid of the man. How dare David treat a creation of God that way! David realized his true problem was with God—David's actions were an insult to God Himself. We need to see every other person as God sees them. That other person might be broken himself, but God wants that other person to come to Him. God does not want to see us take advantage of others or use others. Jesus said we need to love our enemies. We reject God's teaching when we reject others.

Verse 8. David wanted his joy back and compared how he had been feeling to having broken bones. This is what happens when we hide sin and do not confess to get it taken care of—we miss out on true joy in life. We feel like we have broken bones because we are not right. God wants to heal broken people. Sometimes we are those broken people—at times because of what people did to us and sometimes because of what we have done to others. Here, it was what David did to others. God wants to heal everyone involved. Confession and asking for God's healing is where to start so we find joy again.

Verse 10. This is a big request—David wanted a clean heart and right spirit. This is a complete cleaning, and it is needed so that we do not go back to our old sinful ways. We need to be renewed in our spirit, so we do not fall back to the same sin. That is a big request, though. Are you ready for a clean heart and right spirit—to be on a new path? Sometimes we like our old path—David did for almost a year. But it did not bring him true joy and broke his relationship with God. We need to come to God and ask for a right spirit in us to go forward in life.

We are halfway through this psalm. There are more lessons to come tomorrow, but in summary from today, we just need to have a heart that is ready to confess to God and quick to learn from God. I used to coach basketball, and I always looked for teachable players. Are we teachable in life? Can God renew you? He wants to.

Day 36   Lessons from David (Part 10)

Last time, we worked our way through the first half of **Psalm 51**, the record of David's confession for deep sin. Today we will continue. It is good to reread the entire psalm, and I will give some thoughts on a few of the verses. Remember, David did not play games with God—he confessed and called for a complete cleaning of his heart—David wanted God to totally renew him. May that be our prayer too.

Verse 12. David asks God to restore the joy of His salvation. That is a request we need to make a lot, since sin clouds our memory and can dominate our lives. Do you remember your salvation? It was that time you told God you wanted to accept His gift of payment for your sins so you could be with Him—now and into eternity. That is joyful! Two things, though. Have you done that, have you told God you accept Him? That is where the relationship starts. Secondly, sometimes we forget what God did and how much He loves us. It becomes old news, and we lose our joy. Don't let this happen—every day tell yourself the gospel. Here are some verses to help with that. **Romans 5:6–9, John 3:16–17, Ephesians 2:8–9**.

Verse 13. David says that when he gets forgiveness for his sin, he can then teach others. This is very true, and some of you may have opportunities in the future to teach and warn others. David wanted to warn other people not to give in to sin like he did. You will have people in your life that want you to join with them in sin (maybe because you did before). That will be a moment you can teach others and take a stand for God in refusing to join sin. You can have a great influence on others for good in your future.

Verses 14–15. When David got fully right with God, He praised Him for real. He says that when his mouth opens, he will declare God's praise. This is such a wonderful thing to do. Praise God. That happens through our speech and conversation—give God the credit for helping you. This happens in song. Feel free to listen to praise and worship music and even sing along. This happens through prayers in our hearts. We can be constantly praising Him for giving us life and many second chances.

Verses 16–17. Getting right with God is not about how many good works you can pile up. It is about how humble your heart is before Him. David was ready to make sacrifices for sin, but he knew that would not make God happy. God made the final sacrifice for us in Jesus. No, David knew God wants a *broken* (realizes I can't do it on my own; I need God) and *contrite* (humble) heart. We can never do enough good works to outweigh our sin before a holy God, so He is just asking that we acknowledge our brokenness. That is when He can fix us. Think of it this way—I tell my son to mow the lawn. I come home, and he runs out to meet me and shows me some really good pictures he drew. He even made a card for me. Nice. But am I happy? No, because the lawn isn't mowed. That is still a problem until we take care of it. I need him first to acknowledge that he messed up and should have been mowing. This is how God is with us—He is just asking us to see the truth of who we are. Here is the amazing thing—in my lawn-mowing story, after my son asks forgiveness for not mowing, if I was godlike, I would mow it. Wow. My son so does not deserve that—true. But we do not deserve forgiveness from God and blessings from God—yet He can give them anyway. This is why He is worthy of praise.

Verse 19. Now in verse 19, God is delighting in their good works. Why now? Because David had made his heart right before God first. Look at **Ephesians 2:8–9** again and then **2:10**. We were created for good works (verse 10), but they cannot properly happen until we accept the gift of God and be right with Him (verse 8–9). Other religions in the world want people to do good works first, and then if they do enough, God will be happy, but God knew our good works could never match a holy God. Here we see that after we have our heart humbled, then we can do works pleasing to God to show our thankfulness. And since Jesus is our final sacrifice (**Hebrews 10:12–14**), God doesn't want sacrifices anymore—He wants us to be free from those obligations in order to help and serve other people (remember **Galatians 5:13–14**).

Rest in God's forgiveness. Stay humble. Don't take advantage of his mercy (**Romans 6:1–2**) but rest in His love and grace. God wants to forgive us. Wow—very humbling.

Day 37   Lessons from David (Part 11)

Today we are finishing David. There are more stories about his life in the book of 2 Samuel. Unfortunately, a lot of what is left is about the fighting of David's family with each other. David was forgiven from his sin with Bathsheba, but he still had to live with the consequences (**2 Samuel 12:10**) such as lots of fighting among his kids of different mothers (**2 Samuel 13**). But today, we will conclude with a psalm that he wrote so we can see more of his heart when it was good. Overall, we remember that David was bold for God, took a stand for Him, was humble and teachable, and confessed rather than made excuses for his sin. He was not perfect, but he wanted to make things right when he messed up. God gives many second chances!

Psalm 32, 34–41 is a nice run of psalms by David. They show his open heart to God. I will comment on a few verses in **Psalm 34**. Read that chapter first and see if there is anything that stands out to you.

1. (vv. 1–3) David is serious about praising God. He wants to "continuously" praise God. How can we continuously think about God? That would be a noble goal. If you know me, then you know that I continuously think about basketball. I need to be careful and replace that with God. God is worthy of my thoughts and praise. To "magnify" God is to make Him bigger in my life—it is like putting a magnifying glass on God so I cannot miss Him. David had God be really big in His life.

2. (vv. 8–10) These verses claim that God is good and will provide us with all we need. Be careful. Sometimes we think we need certain things, and God knows we do not. This could even be people. Sometimes we really want that person in our life, and it does not happen. This is where we can either get angry at God or we can trust that He knew best. That is hard to do, but God still may have something

or someone better for us in our future. This is faith. Honor God, and He will give what is best for us.

3. (v. 11) This verse is like the third time the "fear of the Lord" is mentioned. This fear is an understanding that God is God, and I am not. He sees me, and I need to remember Him as I go throughout my day. I do not need to be afraid of God, but I do need to respect who He is. That understanding and remembering of God through the day will change how I live. Fear the Lord.

4. (vv. 13–14) Notice there is some good advice in these verses. First, "keep your tongue from evil." If we could just control what we say, that would help us so much. We have got to be slow to speak and quick to listen (**James 1:19**). Too often, we feel we need to shout our opinions or let stupid people know that they are stupid. Instead, we should hold our tongue and let God take care of it all. Secondly, verse 14 says to "turn away from evil" and "seek peace." This also is quality advice. Too often, we play with evil and go places we know are trouble but say, "I will be all right." Well, that is how things turn out badly. We need to make an effort to turn away from bad situations and seek out peace. What can you do today to represent Jesus and promote peace with others? Jesus said to love our enemies—nothing more peaceful than that!

5. (v. 18) The Bible is clear that we need humble hearts rather than hearts full of pride. We just read Psalm 51 and saw that God loves a contrite spirit—one that admits his sin and need of God. But as this verse says, God is near the brokenhearted. Let God heal your hurts and heart. That is hard, but He wants to help you now on this earth to have peace…and wants you with Him for eternity.

6. (v. 19) God keeps it real—we have many problems. God does not say the righteous will have an easy life. God says He will help the righteous through difficulties. Now, since He is talking about the righteous here, the idea is that we do the right thing, and life still goes bad. We still have to

live with the results of sin like David did (see above), but this verse is referring to working through life when I am really trying to live for Him, and still hard times come. Yes, they will come, but God will deliver. Stick with Him.

7. (v. 22) I love that last phrase—"None of those who take refuge in him will be condemned." Commit your life to God, and you will not be condemned. That word means declared guilty of our sin. I am guilty of my sin! But I will <u>not</u> be condemned because I accepted Jesus's payment for that sin. Rest in God, and He will not condemn us. Wow. God is truly worthy of praise. Go forward with the heart of David!

Day 38   Thoughts from Philippians (Part 1)

Over the next week, we will look at just some highlights from the book of Philippians. It is a book that can be very encouraging to keep us looking up, while also challenging us to live out our faith.

Intro—This book was written by the apostle Paul to believers in the city of Philippi (1:1–2). Paul loved these believers and was actually writing from prison under Rome for being a follower of Jesus (1:7).

Read 1:1–14. What specifically does Paul pray for the Philippian believers? How did Paul feel about these people? Here are three big ideas from this passage.

    A.   1:6. God began a good work in you. He will be faithful to complete it. When we first come to Jesus, I don't think we realize how huge it is that we get to live with God from now on and into eternity. He will stay with us. He will always take us back (**Luke 15**). He will do what He promised and carry us into eternity to be with Him. We turn our back on Him at times, but He will be faithful. Not only that, but God is at work changing us right now. He can make us into someone who is very different from who we were before. Isn't that amazing news? When this life is hard, remember that God is still doing His work on us and will do what He promised into eternity.

    B.   1:9–11 is Paul's prayer for the believers. He prays that their love would abound more and more so they can approve what is excellent. In other words, he prays they would have discernment—the ability to make the best choices possible in life (what is "excellent"), and these choices will lead to God's love being spread. Are you choosing the path of love for others? Is your love for others abounding more and more? Those are strong words. We love to live for ourselves, but that is not the challenge Jesus left us. Read **John**

13:34–35. You see, choosing to live this life of love to others is how people will be able to identify us as followers of Jesus. Many religions have symbols, jewelry, and clothes that identify them as followers of that faith. Jesus says that our identifying mark as His followers is love. God wants us to pray that we would love others more.

Notice in verse 11 that as we spend more time with Jesus Christ, we show His fruit more. Jesus said this too—read **John 15:4–5** and **Galatians 5:16–24**. Our goal should be to stay connected to God— to abide in Christ. Let your mind think about the character of Christ rather than the natural desires of our sinful hearts. Spend time learning more about Jesus, and He will shape your character and your being to look more like Him (those fruits of the Spirit). And that means more grace and love to all.

C. Read 1:12–14 again. You realize that Paul really only cared about other people hearing the gospel? That was all that mattered to him. Remember, the gospel is that we are all sinners and deserve eternal separation from a holy God, YET God loved us so much that He provided a way for us to get to Him and made it free for us through faith. Read **John 3:16–18**. Now, Paul is sitting in his miserable prison and says this has actually been a good way for the gospel to spread. Not only that, but others have become more bold in their sharing of the gospel because they see Paul sharing in prison. It is like some people were shy about Jesus, but when they saw how bold Paul was, they started sharing more too. The application of this is clear. You are a representative of Jesus right now and right here (**2 Corinthians 5:20**). Live it out and be ready to gently and caringly share what you believe and why you follow Jesus (**1 Peter 3:15**). Hey, living this way encourages other believers too. I know I am humbled and challenged by men who are reading God's Word and having Bible studies in their pod or dorm in prison today. If you are able to represent Christ there, how can I not represent Him more in my life wherever God leads! This is how Paul encouraged others in Christ. He lived it out and shared the gospel wherever he was.

In summary, remember that however you are feeling today, God sees you and is going to work on you to completion in Him. Show that love of God toward others. Show this true sign of a follower of Jesus—that you love others like Jesus did. And we never love people more than when we are sharing about the gospel of Christ. Look up to Him for strength.

Day 39   Thoughts from Philippians (Part 2)

Today we will do an overview of the remainder of chapter 1. Read **Philippians 1:15–30**. Which verse stands out to you? Why? It can be hard to pick just one verse because there are a number of good life verses here—verses that give our life meaning and purpose here on earth.

    A. Read 1:15–18. What is this talking about, and what is Paul's attitude? Apparently, some people were preaching to get at Paul while he was in prison (maybe to steal the loyalty of a church). But notice that Paul does not care why people were preaching. He only cared that the gospel was being preached. He cared so much about people who did not know Jesus that he did not care who got credit for preaching.

    B. Read 1:19–26. This is a famous section of verses. What do you think it all means? Verse 20 is an excellent life verse since it was Paul's goal with his life. He wanted Jesus Christ to be honored with his life, and he was going to live that way with "full courage" even if it ended in death. That is pretty heavy when you think about it, but Paul decided he would live his life for eternity. That means something. That meant he was not living for money at all, he was not living for comfort at all, he was not living to make friends happy by joining them in stuff that doesn't matter at all, and he was not concerned about having a good time next weekend. His only concern was that people would look at him and see Christ. He wanted Jesus to be honored in his body (this life) no matter what. Actually, he understood death was easier because he would be with Christ, BUT it was not good for others. Others still needed to see Jesus through Paul's life so that is why he said "to me to live is Christ." There is nothing else to truly live for. What are we living for? I feel like God is up there rooting for us because He knows how good this life can be for us, if only we would live for Him. Jesus said this too in **Luke 9:23–25** and **Luke 12:13–21**. May we say with the apostle Paul "to live is Christ." There is no messing around with that statement. Too many of us have wasted days, months, and years of our lives living for what amounts to nothing. Live for Christ.

C. Read 1:27–30. These verses start with a challenge to live our lives worthy of the gospel. What does this mean? I think it means that even though we cannot be perfect (thus, our need for the gospel in the first place), we should live a life that points people to Jesus. I think we have all met hypocrites who say they follow Jesus but live a life opposite His teaching. It is not that we are perfect, but that people can see we are sincere and not hypocritical about what we say we believe. Looking at these verses, there seem to be three results that come from living this life in the gospel. Here they are:

1. "One mind." We are unified together with other followers of Jesus. The world can see our love for others, and we realize we are working together to help people know the true hope that comes through Christ alone. All followers of Jesus are on the same team.

2. Courage. The closer we get to Jesus, the bolder we become. We become more humble and gentle also, but we are not afraid to live for Christ. That is a delicate balance but an important one. We live without fear as we get to know Jesus more, and we also live with more care for others, just like He had. Take courage and be ready to share about Jesus, the one who has changed our lives. (Some verses on these ideas are **Matthew 5:3–10**, **2 Timothy 1:7–12**, **1 Peter 3:13–17**.)

3. Suffering. Verses 29–30 remind us that God never promised peace FROM the world, He promised us

peace from HIM as long as we are IN the world. If we are being a light to the world, we will face opposition (**John 3:19**). That is why we need courage and to be one mind with other believers—together, we can encourage and strengthen each other when we are feeling down (**Hebrews 10:23–25**). God keeps it real with these verses and sends us encouragement later in this very book (read **Philippians 4:4–7**). Be encouraged to live according to the gospel of God. He will carry us through suffering in this life and bring us home to Him (**Philippians 1:6** from last time!).

These verses are deep. Take some time to really think about what they mean in your life and how you can take steps to live for Christ more.

Day 40   **Thoughts from Philippians (Part 3)**

I trust you have been able to find some encouragement in the Lord from Philippians. Today we will look at Philippians 2. Start by reading the whole chapter. Here are a few thought/discussion questions after you read the chapter:

- What verses stand out to you the most?
- What do we learn about Jesus from this chapter?
- How would our relationships with others change if we really followed verses 2–4, 14?
- What can we learn from the examples of Timothy and Epaphroditus at the end of the chapter?

Here are a few thoughts I had in reading through the chapter:

A.   The command (1–4)

God really wants us to be loving and unified in caring for others. Humility is a big word—it means to see the value in other people. It says in verse 3 to count others as more significant than ourselves, and in verse 4, it tells us to look out for the interests of others. How different a place would the world be if we lived this out? I know this is one of the hardest commands in Scripture because I always look out for my own interests, don't you? Yet God's love teaches me the value in everyone else.

B.   The example (5–11)

This is actually a pretty important section of the Bible in telling us about Jesus. Verse 5 reminds me to have the same attitude and mind toward others that Jesus had. He set the example. He was God and yet was willing to set aside living by His power to come help us and show us love. He did not hold on tightly to His "God-ness" but chose to put it aside to become one of us—and not only that, but one of us who was a servant. He allowed us to put Him on a cross! This is quite the example for us. Meanwhile, I get annoyed when my kids want me to do something for them, and I want to be selfish with my time. That is not the example of Christ. He gave everything for us—for us who are not worthy. That makes Jesus worthy of glory and reminds me to give of myself to others like He showed us.

C.   The mission (12–18)

People in the army get assigned a mission—something that needs to be accomplished. The writer, Paul, assigns the Philippian believers a two-part mission here—hold on and hold out! Hold on tightly to your faith and hold out the light of Jesus. The idea of verses 12–13 ("work out your own salvation") is to live out your own salvation—God is working in you (13), so live it out. We live it out by obeying God (12), not grumbling or arguing (14), and holding strong to God's message of life (16). Paul said he lived it out so much that he was pouring out his life like a drink offering (17). That is the idea of having a glass of water and pouring it on the ground—it gets used up—but in this case, we are not holding so dearly to our own life and desires—we are pouring out our lives like that water in service for God. It is the only way to live!

And the reason we are living this way is so we can shine out to the rest of the world (15). We really live in a "crooked and twisted" world. If you look at the world around us, we are encouraged and enabled to think about and live lives that are all about fulfilling our own desires—we are told that we should just do what we want and be true to ourselves without realizing that our natural selves are sinful. God has shown us a path of love and unselfishness through Jesus Christ. We need to show the world that some things are sin and are bringing us down a wrong path. Don't let the world twist wrong into right. May we humbly live our lives in the light of Christ so the world can see a better way. The true way. God's way.

So that is our mission. Hold on to Christ. Don't get sucked into this twisted world's ways. Shine as God's light before others.

Remember Jesus's example for us most of all. He humbled Himself and became us. God became a servant and went to a cross—because He loves us. I know the days are dragging on, but may God give you strength and encouragement.

Day 41   Thoughts from Philippians (Part 4)

Today we will do a deep dive into part of Philippians chapter 3. Take a minute to slowly read **3:1–11**. What stands out to you? Verses 7–10 are famous verses to many—why do you think this is, and what do you think these verses are saying? I will point out a few things to clarify some thoughts in this chapter:

- Notice in verse 1, Paul writes to rejoice in the Lord. At the end of the day, a truly joyful life is found in God alone—and He wants us to have joy; that is why He left us this book.
- "Dogs" in verse 2 is a derogatory word Paul is using to describe false teachers. Paul is quite mad at them because they are saying you need Jesus AND circumcision to be saved (that is weird to us in modern times, but it was a big deal to Jewish background believers back then). Paul was so angry because that is a physical work, and he was saying we are only saved from sin by putting faith and trust in Jesus alone—in *His* work for us, not anything we can physically do. That is why he says in verse 3, we worship by the *Spirit* of God and give all glory to Jesus.
- Then Paul gets personal in verses 4–6 by saying if anyone can list "good deeds" that might count toward getting to heaven, he can. Paul lists them and yet still concludes in verse 7 that all those deeds are loss and nothing in comparison with Christ.
- In verse 8, he says he wants to only know Christ and wants to know Him so much that he considers everything else in his life rubbish ("crap" is actually a better translation of that original Greek word—seriously), so that he can be left with nothing of his own and only Jesus Christ. He emphasizes this again in verse 9—that my righteous standing with God is because of ZERO works that make me look good and

is ALL because of faith in Jesus. Wow. What wonderful news that my future in heaven is not determined by my works, or the family I was born into, or anything like that. It is simply based on accepting the righteousness (goodness) of God offered freely to me because of Jesus. That is the wonderful gospel—good news—of God to mankind.

Now we get to verse 10. Paul says this verse (10) to emphasize one more time that the only way he can get to God for eternity and have eternal life (verse 11) is by Jesus—so he really wants to know Him. A few thoughts about verse 10:

1. The phrase "that I may know Him" carries so much meaning. That was Paul's life goal and can be ours also. Think about what it means to really know Christ. This is much deeper than memorizing facts about Jesus. This is a desire to have a personal relationship with Him and to let Him have His will done in my life, no matter what (knowing that it will be tough but better for me than not living for Him).
2. I want to know "the power of his resurrection." There is nothing more powerful than that. His resurrection brought us life. It conquered death. It allows us to be in relationship with the God of the universe right now and to spend forever with Him after this life. It reminds us how powerful God is—that He is over life and death and all creation, and He is offering us the opportunity to be with Him and to have Him on our side (**Romans 8:35–39**). So, yes, I would like to get to know Him more.
3. Paul also says he wants to "share his sufferings." Wait, Paul says what? He wants to know Jesus so much that he feels he needs to join His suffering, and through suffering, he can know Christ better. Since Christ has conquered death and we KNOW we will have eternity with God, what is suffering for the few years we are on earth in comparison? It is nothing. So Paul wants to understand God more through

suffering. Wow. I might be okay not knowing God that well, right? But God says we are blessed when we suffer for Him (**Matthew 5:10–12**), so suffering is a part of getting to know God. Besides, suffering with God is better than being king of a sinful world. This is how we become more like Him (Phil 3:10). We live for Jesus—He is all that matters. And when people lash out at us, we ~~fight back~~ love them in return because God loves the world so much that He sent his only Son for us. We might suffer, but knowing and showing God's love is worth it. May God give us the strength to live out Philippians 3:10.

Day 42   Thoughts from Philippians (Part 5)

I have been thinking for a few days about the impact of the verses we will read today. I pray that you are well and that God can use His word in your life today. Start by reading **Philippians 3:12–21**. Here are a few introductory questions:

- (12–16) What dominates Paul's life and thinking? Why do you think he lives this way?
- (17–21) Some have fallen away from their faith—why? How does Paul feel about this?

Now a few thoughts on these deep verses:

A. Press on toward the end (12–16)

This is such a great passage. I love the phrase "I press on to make it my own because Christ Jesus has made me his own." That is the gospel. Jesus took me on His team even though I am not worthy. Wow. Well, now that I am on His team, I really want to own this and go all in. That is what Paul is saying here, and now he is pressing toward that day when he will see Jesus face-to-face (verse 14). The apostle Paul lived with a vision of what really matters—God and eternity—constantly on his mind.

There was only one problem for Paul—he had to deal with his past. He had some good things in his past (from 3:4–6), and he also had some bad things, like really bad—he chased down followers of Jesus and beat them, or worse (**Acts 7:58, 8:1-3, 9:1–2** this Saul in these verses is Paul, author of Philippians, before he changed his name). Paul had to live with his past and called himself the foremost (or chief) sinner (**1 Timothy 1:15–16**). We all have some good things in our past and some things we regret. Let's think about that for a minute because Philippians 3:13 tells us that in order to push forward toward Christ, we need to put our past behind us.

If we rest on any good we have done in the past, we become full of pride and cannot see our sin and need for Christ. This happened to the rich man in Mark 10 who said he kept all of God's commandments, which blinded him to the fact he loved his riches more than God (**Mark 10:17–22**). We need to always push to advance closer to God. It is ironic that the closer we get to God, the more we realize how far we are from Him. The closer we get to Him, the more we realize we need to grow more than ever in the fruits of the spirit (remember **Galatians 5:22–24**).

BUT we also need to leave our past. Paul did that by accepting Christ and living for Him. Peter denied Jesus as He went to the cross but found forgiveness in that same Jesus and preached great sermons in the book of Acts. God still used him! Remember this: your past can explain who you are today, but it *never* has to define your future. Jesus can *always* rewrite the ending of the book of your life. Some people look at the past and make excuses. I read this quote in a book last night: "You can make excuses or you can make progress, but you can't make both" (Carey Nieuwhof[1]). Paul could accept that he was a big sinner and confess it because he knew he had a big God. Other people don't make excuses but beat themselves up over their past. Look, Jesus already took that beating for us. He went to the cross to pay for our sins. Payment has been given in full, and it is over. The power of God's grace is that the past does not hold us back. If you are sitting there saying, "But my past is bad and…" then you need to press on toward the grace of God. Grace is undeserved—yes! That is what makes the grace of God toward us so amazing. Take a few minutes tonight, and when you are alone, talk with God. Leave your past with Him—both the good and bad. Let Him know you are ready to "hold true to what we have already attained" (Phil 3:16). He already gave you the victory over your past and your sin. Now it is time for us to hold on to that truth. Paul says that those who are mature will think this way (verse 15). God wants us to hold on to that grace so we can press on toward the day we will be with Him. He wants our life here on earth to have victorious joy, not to be paralyzed by the past. Forget what is behind and go "forward to what lies ahead."

Well, I never got to point B today or the last verses of Philippians 3, so we will move them to next time. May God give you victory and grace every day.

---

[1] Nieuwhof, Carey, *Didn't See it Coming* (New York: Waterbrook, 2018), 79.

Day 43   Thoughts from Philippians (Part 6)

I trust God is guiding you through these days. Today, we start with the last part of Philippians 3 and will cover the first part of chapter 4. Read **Philippians 3:17–4:7**. What are the important points you see? Which verses can apply to your life right now? How can we not worry or be "anxious" according to these verses?

    A.   I see five main points in these verses. We will look at each point pretty briefly but try to find one or two of these points that really speak to you to focus on in your week ahead. First, in 3:17–21, Paul tells the believers to follow correct examples because some people who claim to be on God's team are actually just following "earthly things." This is a serious warning for us—if godly teachers can get sidetracked by things that don't matter ("earthly things," "their belly"—phrases that take away from our spiritual walk with God and emphasize just living for the moment here on earth), then we can certainly get sidetracked easily also. Stay focused and fight your selfish or sinful desires. 3:20–21 remind us that we really belong to heaven, and we should joyfully live with that in mind. We are not alone in feeling these earthly temptations, as we see in these verses, but we need to be alert against them (Read **1 Peter 5:8**).

    B.   (4:2–3) There apparently was some church disagreement, and Paul wanted them to work and get along for the sake of the gospel. This reminds us that followers of Christ will not always get along with each other, but we need to deal with that maturely and come to agreements so that when the world looks at believers, it sees peaceful disagreements rather than explosions, gossip, and division. In this age of social media, we definitely can worry way too much about what other people say or think. Believers in Christ should show Jesus's peace to each other.

C. (4:4) Rejoice. However bad things are for us now, we need to rejoice in the Lord. When we rejoice in Him, we are remembering and focusing on what we have in Him and where we are heading—eternity with Him. **Hebrews 11:13–16** reminds us to focus not on earthly things but on our heavenly home. Sometimes, all we have is our hope in heaven. There is nothing going right for us on earth. Remember that God still sees you and wants you to live now with heaven on your mind.

D. (4:5) *Reasonableness* is the key word. Other translations say *gentleness* or *moderation*. All of these words refer to keeping calm and not doing things in extreme. We have to keep our emotions in control—getting extremely angry makes us feel good for a short moment but has a terrible outcome. Talking gently to people is reasonable and helps get our point across better anyway. Read **Colossians 4:5–6**, **Proverbs 15:1** and **16:24, 1 Peter 3:15**. It is wise to use our words calmly and in moderation. The world today wants us to yell our opinion and argue. Jesus taught and lived with gentleness. This applies to spending money and eating in moderation, etc.—just keeping myself under control in all areas of life because so much of life can overtake us if we don't live in moderation.

E. (4:6–7) These are tough verses to live by. Do not be anxious—do not worry. That is a big command, but it is a command given out of love for us. God knows it is better for us not to live with lots of worries, so He tells us to pray instead. The words *supplication* and *thanksgiving* tell us that prayer is both requesting and praising. We can be bold and free to bring requests to God—He wants us to share our heart with Him and leave those worries with Him. He wants us to remember how He has helped us in the past, and when things don't go the way we want, remember that He is God, and He is trustworthy. I have heard some preachers say that prayer is not so much about changing God to do my will as it is changing my heart to

His. Notice that in the Lord's prayer (**Matthew 6:9–13**), Jesus first emphasized God's holiness and the desire for His will to be done here on earth. Then we let God lead in giving us what we need (daily bread) and having hearts of forgiveness that run from temptation. Praying this way brings us peace (Phil. 4:7). God wants us to be able to face life being at peace. Sometimes we need to not fight for our will as much as praying that our hearts would be ready to accept God's will. Take a few minutes to read through these verses and the Lord's prayer again, and let's ask God for greater understanding of His word, His will, and His peace in our lives.

Day 44   Thoughts from Philippians (Part 7)

Today we will finish up Philippians and close with two big thoughts. First, read **Philippians 4:8–23**. A lot of these verses are personal ones to the Philippian believers, but what two verses stand out to you the most? Why? The apostle Paul had a difficult life. How do you think he got through his days according to these verses? Now, I want to look at two big ideas from this chapter, so here we go:

A.   Be careful with your thoughts (verse 8)

This verse gives eight characteristics (six and then "excellence" and "worthy of praise") of things we should think about ("think on these things"). This is part of the big chain of our lives—ideas become *thoughts*, which become *actions*, which become *habits*, which become a *life*. Think about that—our lives are a series of habits. Those habits started with a one-time action, and those acts often started with some thoughts. God wants us to avoid falls in life, so He says to start at the beginning with our thoughts. We might get bad ideas or sinful thoughts—these enter in. This happens. But then, we must choose to throw them away and feed our minds on better things from the list in verse 8.

This is a two-part activity. One part is to get rid of wrong thoughts. Where do they come from? Bad friends, the media, music (have you heard some of those lyrics?) all can lead our mind to a godless place. The garbage needs to be thrown out. No, really—we need to stop entertaining ourselves with music and shows that only are about sleeping with anyone anytime I want. We need more shows where the hero has one woman, who is his wife, and he is humble rather than busting everyone else's head to prove how tough he is. This is entertaining but not godly entertainment. On the other hand, positive, wholesome, and godly thoughts need to be added in. We get these thoughts from God's Word, Christian music, good friends, quality entertainment. We might need to make some hard decisions about friends or what we watch/listen to, but it is worth it. God says Philippians 4:8 to us not because he doesn't want us to have fun but because He loves us and wants what is truly best for us.

B. Find contentment in Christ (4:11–13)

Philippians 4:13 is a familiar verse, and I love that Steph Curry has written this verse on his basketball shoes. But it does not actually mean that God will help us make three pointers. The context is Paul telling us that he has strength from God to be content when everything is going wrong. He has learned to trust God so much that when physical difficulty comes, Paul is able to stay faithful to God. According to verse 12, this is something Paul had to learn. We do not naturally have contentment or the strength to be at peace when we have needs. Paul learned this over time. So too do we have many needs. So too do we not like how life has turned out for us at the moment. But we can do all things through Christ who strengthens us! Remember that God's grace is there—it lifts us up to stand for another day. God's grace lets us restart. God's grace reminds us that the struggles of this life are very small in comparison to eternity (**2 Corinthians 4:16–18**). These struggles certainly seem big at the time—and they are. But God can give you strength to be content in the worst of times. Be content because you are resting in Jesus and His peace and presence for eternity.

In both of these situations (point A and B) today, we need to focus our minds on Jesus. He will protect our thoughts and give us the strength to make it. He really will. But we do need to have our thinking rooted in God. I think one of the struggles of the Christian life is a simple thing—to remember Jesus throughout my day. Remembering Him through the day helps that godly contentment and strength come. Too often, we are thinking of so many other things that God gets pushed out. Remember to feed your mind on the right stuff (4:8) and to rest on God rather than fight for your own will in bad times. God sees so much more than us, and He is trustworthy. He wants to bring you peace in the midst of struggle. This can really happen because you can do all things through Christ who strengthens you. Remember, He can provide all we need (4:19)—if He is not providing what you need, it may be because you don't really need it. God is working through your difficulties to make you more like Jesus. That is what we all need more than anything else.

Day 45   **Jonah (Part 1)**   Jonah 1

Today we will start looking at a very familiar book in the Bible. Everybody knows the story of Jonah and the whale, right? But there are actually some big lessons we can learn from it. By the way, did this story really happen? The answer to me is pretty simple. Did this world really come from nothing with no God? Was there really no life and then suddenly life? No. I believe there was no life—then God created—then life. So, if there is a God behind this world (and I say yes), then it is easy for Him to step in and break His own rules that He set up for the world and do a miracle. I am absolutely looking at Jonah as an event that actually happened, and we need to look at Jonah as an actual person who argued with God through the book. Okay, with that, here we go. Start by reading all of **Jonah chapter 1**.

So who was this Jonah guy? He was an actual prophet of God who received word from God to go to Nineveh. Historically, we know that Nineveh was the capital of the Assyrian empire, a group of people who conquered a lot of the Middle East and usually treated their captives very cruelly (hence, the logic of verse 2—they were very evil). It looks like God wanted to talk to these Assyrians through Jonah (more on that in a later chapter), and Jonah wanted no part of it. He knew God wanted him one place, and he turned around and got on a boat—umm, Nineveh is landlocked—you can't get there by boat. We see Jonah literally going in the opposite direction from God and where he was supposed to be. By the time we get to verse 5, we see that God was not amused, sent a storm so unusual that the ungodly sailors understood something exceptional was going on, and Jonah was trying to sleep through it all.

Okay, wait a minute. Let's think about what is going on here. Jonah is a prophet of God. He loves his own people and basically is told to go warn his own people's enemies. Jonah says, "Nope." He tries to ignore God by going away and sleeping. Are we ever like this?

- Do we think of others? I mean, Jonah *really* does not care about people from Nineveh. Then again, do we care about people who are different from us? Do we care about other people that have sinned, or do we only want God's grace for ourselves? We are quick to give ourselves a pass, but are we quick to give someone else a second chance? Jonah was a strong "no" on others.

- Do we ignore God? Jonah was sleeping. Sleeping! He was not in a constant argument with God; he was trying to ignore God. Do we ever do that? We might get a thought from the Bible or that we know is from God—it makes us uncomfortable because down deep we do not really want to change (and God absolutely wants to change us!). So rather than saying "I am going to fight against God and disobey Him," we just go to sleep instead. We try not to think about God because we know what He would say to us. That is Jonah sleeping in the boat. He does not want to think about God at all, so he ignores God.

Well, the men in the boat wake Jonah up, and God shows them Jonah is the reason for this big storm. Now, it is interesting that at this point, Jonah does NOT say "I am running from God. I will repent and get right with Him so this storm passes." No, he does not want to get right with God. He rebels to the end and says they will have to throw him into the sea. The men know this means death, and they don't want to be responsible, but in the end, they see no way out and toss Jonah.

Do you see verses 15–16? The storm left so fast that these experienced sailors knew God was at work. When they are confronted with the power of God, they "made vows." That means they understood God at that moment and promised they would follow Him from that point on in their lives. Wow. They were better at following God than Jonah, the actual prophet of God. But that was a big moment in their lives. They really saw God at work and committed themselves to Him. I hope in your life you have a moment where you realize who God really is, and then never forget. Write down the day that you accept Jesus. If you did that but forgot, make a point to pray today and recommit your life to God. Then write this date down. Never forget God. Do not sleep on God. Stay awake spiritually, think about God, and let God teach and guide you. Well, next time we will see what happens with Jonah, but may we think about these lessons from Jonah 1.

Let's continue with the story of Jonah and the lessons we can see from it. Last time we read chapter 1 and left Jonah in the ocean, being swallowed by a great fish. Read **Jonah 2** to see his prayer from inside the fish (which he obviously wrote down when he got out or else his paper would have been wet). There are some important verses in that prayer. What stands out to you?

First, I think verses 2, 4, and 7 are important because they emphasize that Jonah could get right with God. He was driven away from God by his own actions, but God was willing to take him back. Secondly, verse 8 is big because it emphasizes the difference between "idols" and the true God. The difference is His "steadfast love." What is that? It is the fact that God still loves us when we are running from Him and hopes we come back. Idols refers to other religions which are based on works. This is the problem with those beliefs. Do you think Jonah would have had a chance to get back with God in a works-based religion? No way. He was done. But here we see that God still had love for disobedient Jonah. Why is that so important? Because we are all Jonah. We all have had a time where we knew what would be right for us to do in God's eyes, but we chose to ignore God. I mean, we can criticize Jonah all we want (and he deserves to be criticized), but we all act like him at various times. So remembering God's "steadfast love" to a disobedient person (**Romans 5:8**) is really amazing.

Now, can we also say this about chapter 2—Jonah was miserable in the fish (verses 5-6), and the whole reason he got sent there was not punishment so much as God getting his attention so he would come back to Him. God loved Jonah so much that He was not going to let him sin so easily. This is good for Jonah because the best thing for his life at that moment was to get right with God. So God got his attention in a major way. Hmmm. The best thing for us, then, is to be right with God. And if we also are wandering, life might get really hard for us—not because God delights in punishing but because God's steadfast love wants to get us back whatever it takes. When you are going through hard times, it might be that God is trying to get your attention. He does it out of love because He knows coming back to Him is what is best for us. Read **Hebrews 12:5–11** for explanation of this truth. It is worth thinking about.

Okay, Jonah gets spit out of the fish (2:10), and in 3:1–3, God repeats what happened in chapter 1. Same command to go to Nineveh. This time Jonah goes. He has learned his lesson. Maybe. Only maybe because we will see he is still not happy about it. But he does go to the Assyrian capital city (read **Jonah chapter 3** now), which is a huge place (they did conquer a lot of that part of the world back then), and tells them that they have forty days to repent and change, or God will overthrow their empire. Here is the crazy thing—they listen. They actually do repent and look to God. The king says they should turn from their violence. Remember that historically we know the Assyrians felt the best way to keep rebellions down was to let everyone see some torture, and they would shut up. So the Assyrians impaled people on stakes, cut off captives' hands and feet, or gouged out eyes, and other such things (you can Google Assyrian torture and find this out). They were seriously violent. AND YET the king heard of Jonah's message and wanted his people to turn "from the violence" they were doing.

Wait a minute. These Assyrians, out of people in history, really did not deserve to survive another day. They deserved a lot of punishment. But God still offered them another chance. Why? God has "steadfast love" for all people. All people. Who can you think of today who does not deserve to be loved by God? Who did you think of? Maybe someone who wronged you. Maybe some warring world leader. Maybe yourself. Hey, it is true that we do not deserve to be loved by God, but He does care for even us. What a great thing to remember—that no matter how far we have fallen away from God, He still wants us back, and He might need to get our attention for that to happen.

Well, it appears the Assyrians are getting forgiven (they did, but history shows us they went back to their old ways, and around fifty years later, their empire was destroyed), so this should be the end of the story. Assyrians forgiven, people happy, and Jonah happy. Unfortunately, it is not the end of the story for Jonah. God still had to teach him another lesson. Next time.

Today we will finish the book of Jonah. If you remember yesterday, we felt that the book of Jonah should have ended at the end of chapter 3. At that point, the city of Nineveh (Assyrians) repented, and everyone should have been happy, but Jonah was not. He was not happy at all. He was angry. Let's read **Jonah 4** to see what happens next.

The first verse tells us Jonah was "angry" and "exceedingly" displeased. He was *really* upset. And verse 2 tells us why he is so upset—because God is "slow to anger" and has a lot of "steadfast love." He is really mad the Assyrians did not get what they deserve. And this from a guy who ran from God and did not get what he deserved! Jonah never deserved a second chance with God, but God brought him back. Yet his hatred for the Assyrians in Nineveh was so great that he would rather die right now than see the people of Nineveh get saved (verse 3). Wow!

Do you ever get mad at someone else's success? Were there people in school who never studied but got better grades than you? Didn't that make you mad? Maybe even now, some people get out of here while you are stuck in your cell. They didn't deserve to get out before you, right? Our focus is on the other people so much that we forget that God sees us. We forget that it is a good thing that God does not give us what we deserve because we all deserve none of God's grace. Anyway, let's continue.

So Jonah goes out into the sun to watch Nineveh—hoping that it will still be destroyed. Meanwhile, God miraculously grows a plant for shade over Jonah. He does not deserve this but is really happy (only time in the book we see him actually happy). Then God sends a worm to eat the leaves, and the plant dies. No shade. Jonah gets really hot. And bothered. And angry. At God. Rather than realizing he never deserved the plant's shade in the first place, he is so angry with God that he wants to die again. This is quite the temper tantrum. After all that happened, Jonah sees himself as the victim of God's plans to save people. And he is too hot right now. God is interested that Jonah has pity on the plant and thinks he is justified to be angry—even though he did nothing to make the plant grow and give him shade (verse 10). Jonah cares about the plant and himself, but he does not care for the people. So sad. Verse 11 says Nineveh has 120,000 people who do not know their "right hand from their left." What does that mean? It might be a metaphor for right and wrong—the people did not even know right from wrong. Or it means there were 120,000 kids in the Nineveh empire—kids so young they don't know left from right. Doesn't Jonah care about kids? Either way, God is trying to show Jonah how these people were just people who needed another chance. By the way, God ends the verse by saying Nineveh has a lot of cows also. Don't you at least care about the cows, Jonah?

We do not know what happened after that, but we know the message. God loves people and wants us to have another chance. We just seem to not care about each other that much. We get mad at others and just want them to get what they deserve. Yet we don't really want to get what we deserve. This is God's grace. It is for everyone. Let's get to a few lessons:

- When others look bad, assume the best. You don't know the background of that person. You don't know what their family was like growing up. Have compassion.
- God loves everyone and wants everyone to come to Him. Everyone. Even bad people. We like to label people "good" and "bad," but God sees us all as sinners (bad) who need God's love (good). Because of that, we should also be concerned about others and love others. Jonah did not.
- We need God's grace. Jonah forgot in this whole thing that He received a second chance from God. He forgot that God had taken care of him even though he was disobedient.

To summarize the summary: love others, stay humble. Jonah thought he was better than others—nope. Stay humble. Let God lift *you* up and care for *you*. Let God lift up *others* and care for *them*.

When you see someone else in the pod/dorm, remember that God really loves them. That will help us treat others the way God wants us to treat them. And give second chances. We want them, so give them. Jonah—it is much more than just a fish story.

Day 48   Fear (Part 1)

For the next three days, we will take a look at *fear*. What are things that you fear? Are they people, things, or ideas? Maybe you fear nothing! We as people often fear at least two things: change and the future (and lots of changes in the future!). The Bible says a lot about fear, especially about NOT fearing on earth but only fearing God. Today let us look at Jesus's words, specifically from **Luke 12:4–7**. Read those verses and then retell what they are saying in your own words.

A.   Do not fear

In verse 4, Jesus says not to fear those who can only kill your body. Wow, ummm, but that kind <u>is</u> something to be afraid of, isn't it? Still, Jesus understood a couple ideas—first, He understood that this life is only a short time of our existence. Jesus does not seem too concerned about our life on earth, so we should not fear those who can *only* kill the body. Jesus lived with eternity in mind, and thus He did not get worked up over things on earth. For example, Rome was an "illegal" government to the Jews of that day since they were an invading army and empire. Many Jews were upset about paying taxes to Rome (this sounds like a lot of our political concerns today!). Jesus was not (read **Matthew 22:15–22**). He was not living for an earthly kingdom but for eternity, so some things were just not that big a deal—He said pay taxes to Caesar and think about God in everything else. Jesus was concerned about God, not money.

Secondly, Jesus understood who God is. Read Luke 12:6–7 again. Jesus knew that God sees us. Jesus knew that God cares about us. Because of that, He did not see much need to fear here on earth. Do you ever feel like the world is out of control? Do you ever feel your life is out of control? Give both this world and your life over to God. He sees you and cares about you. You are valuable in God's eyes (verse 7). That is so important to our understanding of life and God. You have value, and by giving your life to God, you can experience that value to its fullest (**Matthew 10:39**). It is when we resist God and follow our own plan that we run into trouble. Which brings us to this...

B. Do fear

In Luke 12:5, we actually are supposed to fear someone—God. This reminds me of **Proverbs 1:7**, which says the fear of God is the beginning of wisdom. When we fear God and remember Him, it will change our life. At school, students act better when the principal is nearby because there is a certain fear of that person. Yet if you do what is right, the principal can be a really nice person and friend to students (don't you love remembering your school days? Haha). In the same way, God is wonderful and loves us deeply, but if you are going to fight against God, it is a scary place to be. He is patient but is also just. Too often, people don't live according to godly principles, and when things blow up, they blame God. No, the problem is not God's fault. The problem is that we do not fear God and follow Him—He will direct our paths if we let Him (**Proverbs 3:5–6**).

Note in Luke 12:5 that God does have power for eternity. Again, we need to keep in mind what really matters. This verse implies that so much of what happens in life does not matter. It is really all about getting ready for the next million years in eternity. **Colossians 3:1–5** (and that entire chapter) really says it well. We are already in position to be in heaven with God because of Jesus Christ. Why then would we waste our time and lives with things that do not matter? Too many people are chasing a good time this weekend instead of a good godly life now and a good time in eternity with God. Colossians says to put our minds on things above. God's things—caring for and loving others. It reminds us to stop following the selfishness of our hearts in 3:5 and put away immoral lifestyles, coveting because you want more stuff, and evil desires—put them away and remember God Himself. This is what to actually fear and remember and how to honor Christ. God wants what is best for us—you do not need to fear your future if you know Him. You do not need to fear change because if you know Him, it is often God changing us for the better.

This is what it means to fear God and live for what matters. This life is a gift to us from Him.

May God be your strength today, and may you go forward in remembering Him above all else. That is the joy of knowing God and not living in fear.

Day 49   Fear (Part 2)   2 Timothy 1:7–12

Today we look at a different idea of fear from **2 Timothy 1:7**. This verse reminds us that God is not promoting the fear in our life—it does not come from Him. The more we know Him, the less fear we have. The connotation of the word *fear* here (from the original Greek) is cowardice, and usually we fear/have cowardice because we are afraid of failing, being rejected, and being alone. The answer for fear is in all the things God gives us. He gives us *power* to overcome our fears/cowardice so we can stand for Him and do the right thing. God gives us a spirit of *love* because we need an atmosphere of love in which to thrive. God gives us the power of *self-control* (a sound mind) to believe the truth based on God's word rather than being in a state of panic, despair, and fear. We control ourselves to stay steady in feeding on the truth of God rather than the laws of men, which only lead to fear. Now let's look deeper into all these ideas.

Why do we fear speaking about the things of God? This cowardice is based on acceptance and rejection—what if people reject me because I love Jesus too much? This is fear. Paul tells us not to be ashamed in verse 8. It might lead to some suffering, but it is gospel—good news that this suffering is not permanent because God will carry me all the way to Himself (verse 12). He accepts me. Take some time to think about what that means—think about the gospel (**John 3:16** sums it up in one verse). We do not need to fear because God already loved us at our worst (**Romans 5:8**). It only gets better from here as we rest in Him. This is the *power* of the gospel. It saves us from condemnation and carries us forward to God. Do not fear to be changed in Jesus Christ. We fear change—God's power changes us, and it is okay. Remember that he is changing us for the better to clean up our sin.

God gives us a spirit of love, not fear. We have fear because we have failed or do not measure up to a standard. We think this way with God—that we have to perform and be good enough to get to Him and earn His love, but in reality, we need to *not* live in an atmosphere of performance-based acceptance, which means we are only accepted when we do certain things. Most people treat us that way, and we treat ourselves that way. Unfortunately, we also think that God treats us that way, but that thinking will only lead us to fear and depression because we do not measure up. God does not love us based on *our* performance but based on His performance. He has done the work. We fail and sin, but God still accepts us. That is the true power of love—God's love. Read verse 9. Now read it again. This is God's love.

Self-control shows itself in our life in two ways. One is the self-control to believe God and not believe the lies about Him. Do not listen to the doubts that creep into our head about God not loving us or even Him not being there. God made the universe so we can see the stars and be reminded of the One behind it all. (Read **Psalm 8.**) We also need self-control to make right decisions with our lives. Just because we have received forgiveness of sin does not mean we should keep on sinning (**Romans 6:1–2, 12–14**). Our goal should be a life that honors God. This is why verse 9 says He has saved us and called us to join Him in a holy life. God accepts us as we are but loves us too much to keep us that way. He is working in your life to make you more like Jesus.

So God has not given us a spirit of fear. We do not fear or shy away from representing Him. We do not fear our past because He has taken care of that on the cross. We do not fear His working in our life because it is His holy calling that is at work to chip away what needs to change. You might have some fears in these areas. Maybe you fear going back to old habits that are not good for you—okay, that is a good fear. God can come alongside and take that fear and give you a spirit of power to truly change. You need to stay connected to Him because His resurrection power can change your life (**Philippians 3:10**—remember that verse?). Trust Him to make changes in you that you need.

We have covered a lot today in just a few moments. Take time to really meditate (**Psalm 1:2**) and think about these words—no fear, God's power, God's love, and self-control. This is what can really change our life, rather than us being slaves to fear. God bless as you meditate on **2 Timothy 1:7**.

Day 50   Fear (Part 3)   Luke 5:1–11

This week, we have been looking at fear, and today we see one of my favorite passages in the Bible. Read **Luke 5:1–11**. What stands out to you? Why did Simon Peter react the way he did to Jesus's miracle? What did Jesus's words to Peter really mean? What did this mean for Peter's life from now on?

First, look at what happened—Simon Peter had been fishing all night—he was an experienced fisherman. They caught nothing. There were no fish in that water that morning. Jesus used his boat, taught the people a bit, and told Simon to try again. Simon did not really want to—he was washing his nets (a lot of work!) and knew there were no fish. But because Jesus was this great teacher from God, Simon obeyed—besides, this would show Jesus how much Simon knew about fishing. But somehow, there were fish—a lot of them! Simon Peter knew there was only one explanation—Jesus was God and in control of everything. But that also meant Jesus knew Simon. He knew what kind of person he was. Jesus knew his actions and thoughts that no one else knew. Simon was afraid. He was afraid of God. This seems to be a very legitimate fear. So he told Jesus to leave because he knew he is such a bad sinner. Jesus said to not be afraid! And Jesus recruited Simon Peter to join His ministry team! What just happened?

Simon Peter was rightfully afraid—he was afraid because he knew he had made bad decisions in his life, sinful decisions. And now he was face-to-face with God—God come to earth as a man but was clearly still God. That meant Peter was doomed. Maybe he was fearful because he was hopeless—how can we save ourselves as sinners? Maybe he was afraid because he was ashamed. Certainly at that moment, Peter realized his life up to that point had been less than what it should have been. He admits this—he calls himself a sinner. That is really the right response. I have to realize that I am a person who chooses sin, and because of that, I am not worthy of coming to a holy God. But this is where Jesus says to not be afraid. He came for just this reason—He came to make us worthy of God, not because of ourselves, but Him. And because of that, Jesus could use Peter and told him to follow.

Looking at the story, Peter realized there is nothing to fear in the world but God Himself. But here we see that God is for us, so who could be against us (**Romans 8:31**)? Then there truly is nothing more to fear. We worry and fear about a lot of things in life—none of those things should move us since we are in Christ. God is the only one we should fear—and He says to us don't fear.

Now, I think the scariest thing for Peter would be what happens next. His life is about to be turned upside down. He is asked to leave everything—his fishing nets, his job, his income, his security—and follow this Jesus to be a guy who is fishing to catch men. That is way more scary on so many levels: No security—Jesus better be right about all this. Working with people—people can turn on you much faster than fish can. Besides, most people don't want to change, so they don't want to hear about Jesus. Leaving his job of catching fish—everything would be changed and different for Peter—this is scary, but Peter went along with Jesus pretty quickly. Why? When we understand who Jesus is, everything else becomes small. If we are with Him, what else is there? Truly nothing can keep us down or out of His hands (**John 10:27–29**).

So what are your fears? Do you fear following Jesus—not a little bit of "Sunday morning following" but the real following? Are you ready to be changed and live a totally different life? This is what Jesus asked of Peter, and Peter was so ready to follow. God has led me in my life, and I needed to follow Him—I can tell you that it has always been better. Life is truly better with Jesus. The problem is that we only follow Him a little bit, so we only change a little and only see Him changing our lives a little. Life changes are scary. But listen, it is this same Jesus who is calling you to change your life and fully follow Him. He can be trusted. Simon Peter got a clear picture of who Jesus was—he also got a clear picture of himself. Jesus said follow me. Scared about change? Scared about your life? Follow Jesus. Go all in with Him.

Day 51 God's Way or My Way (Part 1)

Today we will look at **Romans 9:30–10:4.** This paragraph of verses shares an important point about how people come to God. Many people want to be in control of how they get to God and go to Him on their own terms rather than listening to God's rules. We don't like being told what to do. We need to see what these verses say about our way and God's way. First, read these eight verses and see if you can give a two-sentence summary of what they are saying.

Two groups of people are mentioned here. One is Israel—they had a history with God, received the Law in the Old Testament and are failing at keeping it—yet they are still trying to get to God by keeping this Law that they cannot keep. They cannot be perfect like God. They were told about Jesus (the stone or rock in verse 33) but do not accept His path, instead choosing their own. The other group of people is the Gentiles (anyone not from Israel). They were not originally seeking God but found Him and have passed the Jews in their spiritual relationship with God because they accept God by faith (verse 30) and not on their own merits or deeds. This passage describes these two groups of people as those who are seeking to come to God by faith (the right way) and those who are trying to show God how good they are by following some laws and rules (which they cannot keep). There are some important truths for us to see.

1. We are saved by faith in Jesus. This is very clear here— verse 30 shows us the Gentiles were not seeking after God. This means they did not grow up with knowledge of God, nor did they live the "right" way. BUT they found God by faith. They admitted they could not save themselves and go to God that way, so they accepted Jesus and were not put to shame (verse 33). This is us! No matter what our background is, God loves us and wants us. We just need to accept Jesus, accept what God did for us through Jesus.

2. People like their own way. This passage condemns Israel for not submitting to God's way. In verse 3, it says they tried to establish their own righteousness (their own rules) and did not submit to God. Aren't we all like this a little bit—like someone comes up to you with a great idea, but we don't accept it at first because it wasn't our idea? We all have this pride that we want to be first; we want to be in control. The problem is that we do this with God. So many people in the world today say the Bible is an old book and not for me. Why do they say that? It is an excuse for them to be in control of their lives instead of submitting to God—this is exactly what Israel was doing in this passage.

3. People like rules. Now, you would not think this—but we do like rules if we are the rule makers. In verse 32, it says Israel pursued God by works and not by faith. Why might this be? The answer is that keeping rules makes me feel good about myself and increases my pride over those who do not keep my rules. I can say I am better than others. Faith says I am just like everyone else—I need Jesus. I am not better than anyone. Israel had a hard time saying this, and we do too, so we make our own rules to make ourselves feel better than others. No! God gave us Jesus because He loves us all. No one has some works-based advantage with God. May I find my self-worth in the fact God loves me so much regardless of my background. We are never too far from Him—again, verse 30: those who did not seek God at first found Him. Amen!

4. We need faith in what is really true. Some people today say, "Just have faith," but don't say what to have faith in. It matters! I can have faith in my ability to fly and be really sincere and truly believe it, but that won't help me if I jump off a building. In verse 2, it says that Israel was sincere— they had zeal or excitement for God—"but not according to knowledge." So that zeal was pretty useless. They were insisting that they could save themselves and get to God by their own good works and rejected God's plan through

Jesus. This is sad. They did not accept God's knowledge but trusted in their own.

Overall, this passage shows the battle of man versus God. We want things our way even though God's way of faith is much easier than trying to work our way to heaven. At the end of the day, we have to decide if we will let God be God of our lives or not. If not, you will be in control of your life—good luck with that. Why fight God? Christ is our righteousness; we just need to believe and accept Him (verse 4). Then we need to make all our life decisions according to God's way and not ours; God's morals and not ours; God's life goals and not ours. Trust Him. His way is better!

Day 52   God's Way or My Way (Part 2)

Last time, we saw that we need to go to God on His terms and not our own terms. We need to accept His plan and not try to work our way to a holy God, which will never work. It is God's way that leads to life. Once we have accepted what Jesus did for us on the cross, we need to continue to live life in God's way. We need to live life submitting to God's way rather than pursuing our own way through life. It is for our own good! Read **Romans 6:12–14**. This passage really shares just one big idea—Do NOT give yourself over to sin. Let's think about what this is really saying.

1. You have a choice. We have a choice in how to live. It says here to present your body to God. This means while we are in this life, we need to choose God's way and not our way. Submitting to God is possible, but sometimes it involves hard decisions. There might be a group of guys who say to me, "Come hang out with us tonight." Or it might be a girl who says that to me. It might be a good time, but I also know how the night is going to end. Those guys/girls like to party, and it is going to lead me toward sin. I now have a choice. It is my way or God's way. Now, God's way does not seem so fun tonight, but where am I really going with that party lifestyle? Where is it going to lead? Is it really something that is good for me? God knows what is best for us, but the world is calling to us. We need to choose God's way.

2. Sin holds us tight. Verse 12 uses the word *reign*. If we let sin into our life, it will not let go of us. Verse 16 tells us we will be slaves of sin if we go down that path. We will become addicts of sin! This is true. Once we start leaving God's way and following the path of sin, it becomes easier and easier to stay on that path of sin and really hard to leave the sin lifestyle. We truly become addicted to sin. God wants to

free us, but we are going to have to make some hard decisions also. We are going to have to say yes to God and no to our own desires ("passions" in verse 12). These passions represent my way. We need to fight for God's way in our lives.

3. God's grace is ready. Sin does not have to dominate our lives. God is ready to give us His grace so we can be free from the power of sin (verse 14). Wow. That means we can start today. We do not need to work up to a certain point before serving God. We do not need to let our past hold us back from following God's way from now on. That is grace.

4. The fight is now. I am going to be honest. This fight against sin and against my own way is really hard. Each time I give in to sin, it becomes that much easier to give in to sin again. That is why verse 16 warns us about becoming slaves to sin. So when am I going to have to fight against sin? The fight is now while sin is small. The fight is now when the desire to sin is weak because that desire will only grow. The key is found in Romans 13:14. Read **Romans 13:11–14**. We need to live properly by not providing opportunities for our flesh (our own desires and choosing our own way). Here are a few examples: If I know going out with those guys tonight will lead to an opportunity to sin, I need to not go with them. Don't fool yourself by saying you will only party a little and you can control it. No, you are making an excuse to provide an opportunity to sin. The desire to sin will be greater in that situation than now, so say no to sin's desire right now when it is weaker. Maybe I have desires to sin when I am alone and looking at pictures on the Internet. Then when you are alone, don't get on your computer. Get outside and go for a walk or just workout. Do not provide opportunity. Maybe it is that girl. Then you need some distance from her right now. If she is the one for you, then she will honor your choice to honor God by keeping that space apart right now.

Sin is too dangerous, and our desires are too strong when we feed them. In your future, you will have to make some hard decisions, just like all of us do. We all deal with this sinful body that we are living in and need to choose God's way. He is ready to stand with us, but we are going to need to make some strong choices. Remember, God's way is better. It is better to live for God than follow what is mentioned in Romans 13:13. The end of Romans 13:13 is a broken life. The end of choices for God is a peaceful and joyful life here on earth even in the midst of chaos around us. Choose Him every day.

Today and tomorrow, we will do a quick two-part study on the life of Elijah, so let's start by reading **1 Kings 18:17–40**, and then we will break it down.

This chapter is basically a contest to see whose God is the true God by sending down fire to burn up their altar. First, the 450 prophets of Baal (a false god of their day who gained followers by promising good crops) tried to get Baal to send fire—that idea fails since Baal does not truly exist. Then Elijah, as the one prophet of the true God, prays, and God answers miraculously. The people see God's power and actually kill the false prophets of Baal. Interesting. I think we also would love to see God send fire to show His power, but He works differently nowadays. Yet there are still some important lessons here for us.

1. "How long will you go limping between two different opinions?" (verse 21). That is an important phrase. It describes people who are so unsure of what to do that they are limping because they cannot strongly go in one direction or another. Other translations give other nice word pictures of this verse, and in the Bengali language, this is translated as how long will you have your feet in two boats? Have you tried to have your feet in two little boats at the same time? That is a good way to wind up in the water and on an epic fail video! The point is that you cannot go halfway with God and halfway with the world. **1 John 2:15** and **Matthew 6:24** show us that you cannot love the world and God. It does not work, and if we try to serve both, we wind up limping through life or falling in the water. Elijah is mad at the people for trying this halfway service of God and uses the contest to prove to them who they should truly and fully be serving.

Where are you at? Are you trying to stay living in the world and keeping God happy at the same time? You cannot do it. We already have too many hypocrites in the church, and we do not need more. You need to make that decision to accept God **and** to *live* for God, not the world around us. Live for what matters and be "all in" with God.

2. Take a stand for God even if you are alone. In verse 22, we see Elijah is by himself against these 450 false prophets. Yet Elijah is ready to make his stand and try to show the people that God is right. So this is a big deal. I mean, we live in this world, and the fact is that the majority of people in the world are following the false gods of their own pleasure and money. They are willing to say anything to get their way. Are we ready to make godly decisions even if no one joins us? Elijah was, and we need to be ready to stand for God in the face of opposition or derision and people making fun of us for our decisions. Please stay close to God each day so you can be ready to stand against those who might mock you for trying to live a new life in Jesus Christ.

3. Be humble before God and get rid of bad influences. In verse 39, the people bowed in humble worship before God because they saw His amazing power. When we see God for who He is, we should respond in humility. Who are we that God would love us? Then in verse 40, we see the end of the false prophets. Now, this verse is NOT a lesson to kill people today. That was a different era, but the lesson of getting rid of bad influences remains. When we see God for who He is, we need to be humble and get rid of those influences that would draw us away from God. Run from things or even people that want to draw us back into our previous lifestyle. Make that stand for God.

Conclusion: Where are you in this story? I would like to quickly answer that obviously I am Elijah, but if I am honest, I think we all start as prophets of Baal. We are in the crowd, and we are not ready to take a stand out on our own. Maybe we don't have the faith yet that God will take care of us if we leave the crowd. But we need to get to the point where we can be Elijah. We need to be ready to stand, even if we are alone. We need to get rid of influences in our life that bring us away from God. We need to stop limping around trying to please ourselves with all the world offers while trying to serve God at the same time. Can't be done. We need to give ourselves completely to God and stand for Him. He will show Himself faithful to us, just like He did with Elijah. Trust Him. Each day, do something to get closer to God. Pray and share your heart. He has got you just like He had Elijah.

Day 54   **Elijah (Part 2)**   1 Kings 19

Have you ever been discouraged? Depressed? Felt alone? It is pretty frustrating to feel that way and can really put us in a bad spot emotionally and spiritually. Actually, we often have very good reasons to be depressed. The problem is that when we are controlled by depression and discouragement, we are not letting God work in our lives like He can. Yesterday, we looked at Elijah's victory over those who did not believe God was truly God. Today we will see a quite different story. Read **1 Kings 19:1–18**.

Note what happened. After such a big victory in the previous chapter, Elijah thought everyone would turn to God. Instead, a death warrant is put on his head (vv. 2–3), so he runs into the wilderness. He moans that he is the only one who is staying faithful to God. Meanwhile, God asks him why he is in the wilderness (v. 9) or, in other words, why isn't Elijah doing his job of preaching among the people? Elijah again defends himself by saying he is the only one left who cares about God. God then gives him instructions to anoint his replacement (v. 16). Interesting. Very quietly, Elijah just got fired. Lastly, God says a kind of "by the way" statement of "I still have seven thousand people who are faithful to me." So ummm, Elijah you are not the only one left on God's team after all. He felt that way, but God still was at work. What can we learn from this story?

1. Depression often happens when our expectations fail, or we think we are the only one and alone. Elijah thought everyone would join him on God's side. His expectation was crushed, but he also thought he knew the whole story, and he did not. He thought only about himself, not realizing God was at work in the lives of seven thousand people. God does not need to tell us His every move or plan. That is why we need faith that God is at work when we don't see it—because He is. Do not lose hope. Please know that whatever situation you are in, God can work through it

and may already be working in ways that you do not know. This is trust and real faith—doing the right things when we don't see how it will end.

2. Don't go there. When Elijah got down, he left where he was supposed to be and went off by himself into the wilderness. This was just the moment he needed to be around other godly people, but he left them. Be careful about going away from God's people. Stay near them. Do not go to a place you should not be at when you are feeling down. This happens all the time in society. On TV, people go to the bar when they are down—this is the perfect time and place for bad decisions to be made. It says "I am in a bad mindset, so I am going to lose touch with reality in a bar with other people who are losing reality so we can all make drunk decisions together." And then we wonder how things went wrong. Well, this is what Elijah did—he did not go to the bar, but he got away from anyone who could help him and kept telling himself this false reality that no one else was on God's team and that he was going to die because God could not protect him. Not true! Elijah needed to go to God—fortunately God came to him. Look, when you are feeling down, go to God. Go to prayer. Go to God's people. Fill your mind with His truth.

3. Trust God's facts and not your feelings. A successful life is lived by doing things we do not want to do in order to get where we do want to be. No kid feels like going to school every day, but every kid needs to go in order to learn. We don't feel like getting out of bed, but we need to. Elijah did not feel like staying around God's people, but he needed to. Elijah did not feel God was treating him fairly, but God was actually at work a lot. You may not feel like talking to God each day, and you may feel down today, but trust God's facts. God does see you wherever you are (FACT—**Proverbs 15:3**). God loves you more than you know (FACT—**1 John 4:19**), God loved you enough to die for you so you could come to Him simply by accepting His

payment for your sin (FACT—**John 3:16, Romans 5:6-9, John 1:12**). We don't feel new every day, but God wants to recreate us in His image and help us be new people in Him (FACT—**2 Corinthians 5:17 and 3:18**). So yes, we do feel down and depressed sometimes, but do not let those feelings overwhelm you from God's truth. Go forward in His strength and encouragement. Accept Him and rest in His truth.

Parables of Jesus
                        (Part 1)

What is a parable? It is a little story that Jesus told to help us under-stand a spiritual truth. We like stories. They help us pay attention, and sometimes, we even learn something from the story. Jesus under-stood this, and He used these "teaching stories" a lot. We will take a few days and look at some of His parables to see what we can learn. Today, we will see a very important principle that Jesus taught, so to begin, read **Matthew 20:1–16**. What do you think is the main lesson Jesus wants us to learn from this parable?

The story: So this wealthy landowner went out to hire workers for his vineyard. In those days, there would be a street corner where available workers would sit waiting to get hired for a job. The master hired some guys early in the day and agreed to pay a denarius, which is a day's wage. Seems very fair. As the day goes on, though (third hour would be like 9:00 a.m.), he hires more workers saying he will pay them what is right. Finally, he goes to the street corner at the eleventh hour (one hour before sunset, like 5:00 p.m.), sees guys still needing work that day, and hires them to work until sunset. Then evening came, and he starts paying everyone a denarius. This is very generous for those who did not work a whole day. The morning guys then also get a denarius and are a little upset, but their pay was fair. The story concludes with the master telling those guys, "I was com-pletely fair to you. Can't I choose to be generous with some of my other money?"

Lesson 1: God is fair, or more than fair. He is not unfair.

The workers from the morning agreed to work for one denarius. What did they get? One denarius. What do you deserve from God? We like to compare ourselves to other people who are worse than us (or so we think) and say that we deserve more good things from God than someone else. The sad fact is that we are all sinners (**Romans 3:23**) who deserve nothing from God. Wow. We must remember that God treats us very well. We cannot say "I deserved more from

God because I was so good." Only God is good, and He is not unfair to us. If He was truly fair to us, we would be in trouble.

Lesson 2: We are all the last workers. Embrace God's grace.

As I just wrote, we like to think of ourselves as having some points with God. We don't. The Bible says our righteousness is like filthy rags or a polluted garment (**Isaiah 64:6**). The fact is that God loves giving grace. He is offering us eternity with Him—that is so undeserved. This is the very definition of God's grace—that we get something we don't deserve. Realize that we are all like the eleventh-hour worker who received a lot of God's grace. This is such good news to us too—God cares even for those who come to Him later than others.

Lesson 3: Are you okay with others receiving grace?

Here is actually the main lesson. Jesus told this parable because some people thought they were better than others. Some people look down on others and think, *They do not deserve the same as me.* What does Jesus say about this? He hates it. He loves giving grace to undeserving people. Are you okay with other people being blessed, or do you just want yourself to get everything and no one else to get anything? If we are honest, we do have these tendencies to just look out for ourselves. We have to trust that God knows what He is doing when others get blessed more than us because we do not know the whole story. And besides, why are we so concerned with what everyone else is getting? God scolded those nosy people through this parable. But we do have to remember that others in our life who we do not like—we need to turn them over to God, and if they repent and receive God's grace too, that is great. Are you okay with grace for all and not just you? We all struggle with this but need to see people through God's eyes of grace. Remember that we are not in a race; we are under grace.

Where are you at with this story? Have you accepted God's grace, or does it make you mad that God offers His grace to that other guy too? Stop it. We do not know that guy's story. Let God deal with him. We each need to personally accept what Jesus has done for us without worrying where others are in comparison to us. We are all at the bottom, and God reached down to lift us up through Jesus. That is truly good news from God for everyone.

Day 56   **Parables of Jesus**   The Good
                     (Part 2)   Samaritan

Today, we will look at one of the most famous of Jesus's parables, the Good Samaritan. Read **Luke 10:25–37**. Notice the context—a lawyer wanted to "justify himself" (v. 29), so he asked who his neighbor was. In other words, this guy was kind to his neighbors who were all wealthy or "religious" like him but did not care about other people. So he wanted to justify himself by saying that only some people are my neighbor, and I am kind to them—but those who are not my neighbor or like me, I don't care about. Jesus's point was to show how important everyone is. Some lessons:

1. Religious knowledge is nothing without action.

The parable was about loving your neighbor—and showing it. The question was who was the true neighbor to the stranger? The last guy, of course. But who were these first two men who passed by without helping? They were a priest and Levite—religious people! Those two men represented those who knew all the answers and looked good in society. They would look good in church! But when they left worship and weren't in the temple, we see these two not even care about the man. They see this guy and go to the other side of the road! Wow. Jesus specifically shows these men to call out those who talk a good talk about religion but do not live it out.

Where are we at with this? I think we can all talk a good game, but how are we showing our faith in Jesus? Do people look at us and say there is something different about us because we care about others? That is what Jesus calls us to here. He wants us to live out our faith that says God is full of grace to everyone. Take a minute. What are some ways that you can show God's grace and love for your neighbor when you get out? Okay, now an even bigger question: what are some ways you can show care for your neighbor right now? That would make everybody's time here better, wouldn't it? Wherever we are, let's tell others that we know Jesus, and show it.

2.   My neighbor is everyone.

The fact is that God loves everyone. We know this. But if that is truly true, then we need to treat other people as though they are someone God really loves. Everyone. This is hard. It is easy to show kindness to kind people, but to do that to people who do not deserve it is hard. But, remember, that is what God did for us—He loved us while we were still sinners and unlovable (**Romans 5:8**). This guy in the parable was pretty beat-up. He needed a neighbor, and the Samaritan became that friend, which brings us to this.

3.   There can be no racism in Jesus's kingdom.

Jesus was a Jew talking to Jewish people. The Samaritans were a people group the Jews of that day hated (and vice versa). History is full of people groups who hated each other, even today. Jesus is making a big point when he says it was a Samaritan who helped the guy. Jesus is smashing racial stereotypes and saying people are people, no matter what. Jesus was consistent about proper treatment of the Samaritans. Look at **Luke 9:51–56**. Jesus's own disciples were pretty quick to suggest the destruction of a Samaritan village. Jesus scolds them. No. Look, we need to get past who people are and just realize that people are people, and God loves us all. Followers of Jesus need to be leaders in reaching out and caring for people who are different from us. Jesus wanted these people to see that the Samaritan in the story was willing to show love and care for someone his village hated and hated them back. Jesus is showing what He did for us.

You see, everything comes back to the cross. Jesus saw us in our sinful condition. And yet He cared enough to go to the cross for us. That changes everything. I do not know what you are struggling with today, but I know that God cares just like that Samaritan did. It sounds like trite words, but it is true. Accept that care and concern from God and let Him take care of you. You see, that is part of it too—sometimes we don't let God care for us. He wants to. Let Him change you.

So there we have this famous parable. Remember to let God help you and then go and be that Good Samaritan to someone else. Who around you needs a friend? Who needs to know God's peace? May we all be examples of loving our neighbor today.

Day 57   Parables of Jesus   Matthew 13
(Part 3)

Today, let's look at two big ideas from three very short parables. And just to repeat, these are really big ideas.

1. What are you living for? (**Matthew 13:44–46**)

Have you found the meaning to your life yet? You know that you are living for something, right? I mean, we all live for something or someone, whether we realize it or not. If we do not realize it, then we are probably living just for ourselves. Either way, has your life brought you meaning thus far, or are you still searching for that something that brings meaning to life? Some people go "all in" living for something (or somebody) and find that it (or she) doesn't bring the meaning to life that we thought it (or she) would. Others try to have it both ways—like maybe we know that we should live for God, so we do a few little "God things" on Sunday but actually live for ourselves the rest of the week.

That brings us to these parables. In the first one, the man finds a treasure in a field, which is so valuable that he covers it up so no one buys the field before he does and "sells all that he has" for that treasure in the field. The second parable is just like it. A merchant is traveling looking for pearls and finds the mother of all pearls. When he finds it, he "went and sold all that he had" in order to have enough money to buy that one pearl of great value. The kingdom of heaven is like this. Finding God is like this! This is finding the true meaning of life—it is God and His kingdom. And what is that worth? What is following God and His kingdom worth? It is worth everything you have.

Okay, let's talk real here. I personally believe there is only one thing to live for. It is God. God is what matters, and God is who counts for eternity and now. He offers us eternal life by simple faith, though we don't deserve it, AND He shows us how to live right now here on earth. Following the teaching that God's book gives us is the best way to live. Jesus talked all about living out His kingdom here on earth in **Matthew chapters 5–7**. If we follow this, we would have a more peaceful life and meaningful life. Jesus said it is all about loving God and loving others. Yes! The problem is that we put ourselves into the mix. I try to live for God some and myself some. We all do it. That is when I mess up—when I try living for myself and add some God to that. No. These parables show us how living for God is worth EVERYTHING we have. He really is. I would encourage you to go "all in" with your life for God. He truly is worth our all.

2.   You have potential with God. (**Matthew 13:31–32**)

This is a short parable, or simply teaching, that compares our faith and life with God to a mustard seed, which starts off as a tiny seed but grows up into a large tree, so large that birds can make their home in it. This is a picture of our faith journey. First, we hear the gospel, the good news that Jesus died for our sin. We may not understand much beyond that, but if we understand that much, we can accept Him and with that faith start our life with God (**John 3:16, Ephesians 2:8–9**). Now we might not think that much will change, but our life can then change A LOT. What started in a small moment of faith in God can blossom into a new way of living and a new "you." Jesus told this parable because He wanted us to see that any of us that come to Him can make something of our life with Him— actually, it is God changing us so much that we can be a blessing to others, just like that tree had birds make their nests in it.

Do you think God can do something with your life? The answer is yes. You have potential. God can take your life and make it glory for Him. Each day, we submit and seek Him, and He will change us. Each day, just do the next right thing—God can take that and make a life. You can be used to change other people and restore relationships and show others that they can have hope in this world in God. Do not sell yourself short and say that God can never use you. No! It starts with a small bit of faith, of trust in God that He will guide you as you make the next right decision in Him. Jesus's teaching was clear, and by the way, He used these disciples of His to change the world. His disciples were not perfect and made some bad mistakes along the way, but they trusted Him and wanted to follow Jesus. Jesus took that small faith and changed them into leaders for God.

Hey, go all-in with God. Put your faith, however small it is, in Him. He can and will change you for the better and bring you home to be with Him in the end. Nothing is better. Jesus is the treasure.

Day 58   **Parables of Jesus**   Matthew 25
                          (Part 4)

There are two parables to read in **Matthew 25**. One is verses **1–13,** and another in verses **14–30**. Read them. What do you think they mean and what do you think are lessons for us?

A. The stories

The first one deals with some customs of their day that we don't fully follow today, but we do know there is a wedding feast, and some girls were wise and prepared for it, while some were foolish and unprepared and missed the chance to join. The bridegroom only took with him to the wedding party those who were ready right when he came. In the second parable, a man leaves "talents" (probably a unit of money, not ability) with his servants while he is gone, and two of the servants invest and work so the talents double. One did nothing and merely gave his talent back. Again, the theme is that two did what they were supposed to and were ready when the master came back, while the other one did not work and was not accepted when the master came back.

B. The lessons

1. The first clear lesson from these parables is that *we should be ready to meet our Maker*. We do not know when Jesus will come again or when we will die and meet Him, but we better be ready. The good news is that God has done the work and paved the way for us to be ready to meet Him. It is through accepting Jesus's payment for sin (**Romans 5:17–19, Romans 10:9**) that we can be made righteous and be accepted by God. Now, when we do that, we are saying that we cannot save ourselves. Some people do not want to admit that. Some people look for excuses to keep

living like they want instead of giving their heart to God, even though it would be better for them. Some people say they will think about it and make a decision about God later. All of these are excuses and ways to soften their NO to God. That is what this first parable is about. The foolish ladies did not prepare, became lazy, slept, and ran out of oil when they needed it. They did not take the bridegroom seriously. Too many people in this world are not taking God seriously. He loves you, but He will leave you behind if you try to get to Him without accepting His payment for you through Jesus. Be ready.

2. Second lesson: *Use your time wisely*. I hope and trust you have accepted Jesus. So now what? Use your time for Him. There is a clear principle in both these parables about working now before the Master comes. That is a picture of our lives on earth until we meet God. What are you doing with your time? Take a moment and think about what you want your relationship with God to look like. It begins with God because a right relationship with God will lead to a right relationship with others and will lead to a good life here on earth. How can you improve your life with God?

Are you ready for the day you get out of here? Let's be honest, statistics show that many people who go to prison return. We need to let God break that cycle. God has got to be a bigger part of our lives. We need to use even this time wisely. Now, I know that is hard since the pod/dorm is loud with the TV on, people talking constantly, and games happening (arguing). But you need to use this time to make habits in your life that you will keep with you on the outside. Specifically, we are talking about acknowledging God in your life every day through prayer time, reading and/or meditating on God's Word, and taking time to positively think about where you are going in life. Get those habits into your life. Fill your mind with God's thinking that comes from His word. Make plans to succeed in the future.

I used to coach basketball. During timeouts, we would talk about what the opponents' weak spots were and where we wanted to attack. In other words, I wanted my team to have a conscious plan each trip down the court. We needed to keep the goal in mind at all times. In practices, I reminded them that "practice makes perfect" is not correct. "Practice makes permanent," so only perfect practice makes perfect (then I yelled at them about what they were doing wrong in the drill). We are beings of habit. We need to make the practice of acknowledging God permanent in our lives. God needs to be permanent no matter where we are. Each day, we need to live like Jesus lived. These parables tell us to not be foolish with our time but wise for God. Do what it takes to make God bigger in your life now so that those habits stick with you in the future.

Day 59 **Parables of Jesus** Matthew 18
  (Part 5)

I trust you are having times with God right where you are. Get in that habit of looking to God each day. He sees you. Now, since we are covering parables, we have to cover this important parable about forgiveness. That is a big topic that touches all of our lives. First, read what Jesus said in **Matthew 18:21–35**. What are your thoughts about this passage? A couple things that stand out to me are (1) Forgiving is hard! Peter thought he was being a good guy when he offered to forgive someone seven times. It turns out Jesus asks us to forgive more than that. (2) We don't like forgiveness unless we are receiving it. The guy in the parable was desperate to be forgiven of his debt that was too huge for him to EVER pay back, but when someone else owed him a far smaller amount, he had no desire to give forgiveness. If we are honest, we feel that way too. We do not want to offer forgiveness, we want our money back or our honor back, at least until we mess up, at which time we are very much for forgiveness and are grateful to be forgiven.

So I want to take a few thoughts today from Pastor Mark Driscoll on forgiveness and will write some of his ideas below in quotes because forgiveness is the core of Bible teaching. Jesus came to earth for us so that God would forgive us. Jesus tells us to forgive because we have been forgiven. What does this mean in practical life?

Forgiveness IS:

"Both a one-time event and an ongoing process." That is so true. We can say the words, but we still need to work through the process of giving up that hurt and that person to God.

"Not keeping a record of wrongs." We choose to box up that event and put it away.

"Giving up control of the outcome." We forgive and let God take care of any revenge, not us.

"Choosing health for our body and soul." We have to release hurts to God, or they will keep us down.

Forgiveness is NOT:

"Denying or pretending nothing happened." We need to address the situation in order to move on.

Trust. We can forgive now, but "trust is gained over time," so there is wisdom in being careful. Some relationships are not good for us. We need to forgive but still move on.

"Based on their apology" That other person may not say they are sorry, but I still need to forgive them in my head and before God, for my own sake. If we don't forgive, we will do something like they did to us, and then we have just become the one who hurt us.

What happens if you do not forgive? I will list two things here that show why we should forgive:

- Bitterness. If we hold that grudge against the other person, we become old and bitter. We stay angry. We are not a pleasant person. "Today's anger is not a problem. Yesterday's anger is a problem." Do not let that anger grow because...
- War. "When two people are at war, they enlist armies." We start telling other people about our issues and force them to take sides. Then we have an entire group against another entire group because there was no one who stepped up and forgave. Now everyone is involved.

Why should you forgive? Now we are back to the parable. We need to forgive because God forgave us. We need to forgive because we are not perfect, and someday *we* will also need forgiveness. The Bible is clear that God is holy, and we have sinned against a holy God. Yet He forgives us through Jesus. This is so huge! We need to realize that we are that guy in the parable with a debt that is so huge we can never pay it back to God. So when He forgives us, He tells us to do that to others and forgive. Read **Ephesians 4:32** and **Colossians 3:13**. Both these verses tell us to forgive as God forgave us. It all comes back to that. We are never too far from God's forgiveness, so be willing to forgive others also.

I know this is hard. I know we can stay up at night thinking about that person who did us wrong. I know. But I only have two options. Revenge and bitterness, or forgiveness and peace. You see, forgiveness is the way that I get peace. I need that peace so I can sleep! I need to give that other person over to God and let Him take care of the situation. I need to remember the forgiveness I receive in Christ and rest in Him. May God strengthen you in this important area.

Mark Driscoll quotes are from his sermon notes found here: https://realfaith.com/finding-freedom-through-full-forgiveness-win-your-war/.

We are going to finish our series on parables with the very important chapter of Luke 15. First, read **Luke 15:1–7** and **11–32**. What are the three lessons you see from these two stories?

The lost sheep: Think about what is happening here. The shepherd has ninety-nine out of his one hundred sheep safe at the end of the day. That is great. Imagine getting a 99 percent on a test at school. I would be pretty happy. But this shepherd wants that one— that one that couldn't just stay with the other ninety-nine sheep— that one that did not listen—the shepherd wanted to go find *that* one. Hmmm. The shepherd, of course is Jesus, and we are that one sheep. We are the ones that need to be rescued and saved, and God is willing to do that. Wow. Jesus wants us to know that God's love for us is willing to chase us down. Just accept Him.

The prodigal son: This is a famous parable with many lessons. Notice the prodigal son spent all his money on "reckless living." I find this important because the world is offering us a good time in reckless living. The world says, "This is all you got so live it up. We should try stuff—just one time is no problem. This is fun. She is fun. Don't worry about it. Everything will work out." These are the lies of the world. The prodigal son found out that this is not wise or honorable living, and he wound up as a servant feeding pigs. He actually totally got what he deserved, but this is where the story takes a twist. Let's look at lessons for us from the three main characters here.

1. The son: He made many bad decisions in the story, but he did make one good decision to go back to his father. He realized he had no other option and was willing to be a servant in his father's house. How about us? Do we turn to our heavenly Father? Some people are very stubborn in their ways, and even when they have hit the bottom, they refuse to look to God and blame Him instead. This son

realized he could only blame himself and humbled himself to go home.

2. The Father: One big lesson with the Father, right? He loves us and wants us—even when we are at our worst, He accepts us. Even when we have turned on Him, He takes us back. This parable is all about how God loves us so much that He will accept us when we are at the end of ourselves. This actually might be hard for us to accept, since we know we do not deserve to be accepted by the Father, but that is the main point of this parable. God loves me and you that much.

3. The brother: Okay, so there are lots of lessons with the brother. Here we go:
   - He was mad his brother got forgiven because he did not deserve it. Are you okay with other people getting God's grace when they don't deserve it? This is the heart of God's gospel—He says it many times; that is why we had this same lesson in a parable I wrote about the other day also. We need to be okay with others getting God's grace, especially because...
   - We all need God's grace. Somehow, this brother thought he was better than the other son. Maybe he was outwardly at this moment, but this brother forgot those times that he sinned and that he needed the father's love too. May we never think we are better than someone else because we did not do the same kind of sin that they did. **Romans 3:23** reminds us all sin is sin and puts us short of God's perfect standard. We all need the Father.
   - The father told the brother, "Son, you are always with me, and all that is mine is yours." That is a big statement. Do you realize what we have in God? Way too often, we are like this brother who does not even realize how wonderful it is to be close to God and have a good relationship with our Heavenly Father. God is offering such peace and purpose and guidance

through life to us, but too often, we are just looking at others and thinking, *Why did they get that?* The prodigal son got mercy and acceptance. The brother also had mercy every day; He was near the Father every day! Do not take lightly the fact that the closer we get to God in this life, the more He can give us inner quality of life. He wants us to be joyful through life. Embrace Him.

Luke 15 is about God's mercy. He is offering it to you today through Jesus Christ, who paid for our sins. If you are not close to Him, come back. His arms are open, and He wants to offer you the best gift ever: Himself. The opportunity to live with the One who loves us most.

Day 61　　　　　Titus 3:3–7

Today we are going to look at a few important verses in the back of the Bible. **Titus 3:3–7** gives us a little overview of what the Bible is truly teaching in just a few verses. They tell the story of us. Read this passage.

1. Wow, verse 3 really keeps it real. It describes us before we met Jesus. What stands out to you from this verse? I think of that phrase that we are slaves of our passions (what we want) and slaves of pleasure. It is like we pursue pleasure so much that we have to pursue it more and more because the world's pleasure doesn't last, and just like that, we are slaves to our passions. Also, the end of the verse stands out in saying a whole bunch of the world is hated and hates others. That also is keeping it real with all the conflict we see in the world today, and the conflict that we find ourselves in with those close to us (or who *were* close to us). Basically, this verse shows that without God, this world is not a pretty place, and neither are we. We need God because we are "foolish" and "disobedient."

2. I love the wording of verse 4, especially the word *appear*. It is like in the midst of all this hatred and futile chasing after nothingness, out of nowhere, what should appear but the goodness and loving kindness of God. Here we are slogging it out in the mud of this world, and yet God still loves us enough to make an appearance to save us. That appearance, of course, is Jesus (the personification of God's love) who came to pull us up out of the mud of this world. This is why it says that our Savior appeared. A Savior saves. We are saved from something. So we see how we pursue the world's answers for life in verse 3, which leads to selfishness and hatred until Jesus comes along and shows us some-

thing better, saving us from the futility of this world. This is God's kindness—truly undeserved. Yet He loves us.

3. In verse 5, we see what happened when we were saved. A lot of people think they are saved because they have been pretty good. We like doing good works because we like getting points. We go to church or say a prayer in hopes of getting points with God without realizing that we have already been tossed out of the game because of our sin. This is why verse 5 tells us it is not of our works, however good they may be. We are already disqualified because of sin. But somehow, that is okay because God is full of mercy! That is why God wants to save us—because He cares for us and does not want to give us what we deserve. So when we accept Jesus, God saves us. It is that easy and simple because He loves us. (By the way, **Romans 10:9** does remind us that this means we are giving our heart to God—that we truly believe in our heart and are not just playing the game of saying the right words as another good work to get good with Jesus. God keeps it real with us in how He wants to save us. Let's keep it real with Him.) Titus 3:5 says that when we turn to God, He washes us clean by the power of His Holy Spirit. Amen.

4. This little passage concludes with verses 6–7. They are overwhelming. We were so far from God in verse 3, and now just a few verses later, Jesus is richly giving us true life: eternal life. It says we are justified by grace. That means when I turn to God, He sees me just as if I never sinned. That is to be justified in His sight—I am made worthy of being with God, and now the end of the story of my life is eternal life with Him. How am I made worthy? It is that grace of God. Grace is like my kid—I tell him to mow the lawn by the time I get home, and he doesn't do it. This is a problem. He turns to me when I get home and says, "I am sorry. I failed. Forgive me." And I show him grace by forgiving and bringing him out to the ice cream shop. He deserves nothing from me, but I accept his heart that is

broken over his failure to mow. And that is God with us. We do not deserve eternal life, but God accepts our heart that is broken and sad over our own failures and sin. He shows us grace.

We can never forget what we have in Him. We can never forget God's grace and mercy to us and the gift of Jesus Christ that has been given to us. This right here is why we get up each day. May God use your time here to hammer home the message of the Bible. May we be stronger men in God and His truth a few weeks from now than we are today. Rest in the joy and peace of God's goodness. Let's never go back to verse 3 and always stay in the truth of verse 7.

Day 62   All Things New

Imagine that you get a new car. It is a car you bought from a friend who says he hardly drove it. The car looks great—original paint, original engine. Then you drive it a few days. You notice a chip in the paint and a different color underneath. The engine starts making noises, and you see the parts are not as new as you were told. A few months later, all you have left is an old clunker. The car wasn't really new—it was just shined up. That new car shine will only last so long before the true nature of the car is revealed.

This is a story that parallels our lives. Many times, we try to put a new shine on our lives—we make new decisions and outwardly look great, but inside, we have not addressed the big question of what are we truly living for. We have not solved some of our true and deep issues, but we look good for now. The days go by and old habits come back since we haven't replaced them with new activities and new mindsets. Maybe we are trying harder, but our heart hasn't changed, and we haven't truly gotten right with God. Then we are just like that old car that looks new for now, but underneath? Nope.

What does God really want to do for us? He wants to make us new. He does not want to shine us up; He wants to replace old desires, old goals, and old activities with a new focus and a new direction toward Him. **2 Corinthians 5:17** says if we are in Christ (we have to be in Him), then we are a totally new creation. We are a new person. That is a deep change. Notice it says that the old has passed away. We are beyond those old ways of living and are fully changed. This is a big deal, and this is what God is calling us to. If we are honest, a lot of us want to be new. So what is up with that? Three things to remember:

1. "Born again" means totally new. God has never called us to a small change from who we were. He has always said we can be totally new in Him, but we must be reborn (**John 3:3**). Too many people try to add a little bit of God to their

activities, which leaves them shiny on the outside but the same on the inside. Jesus wants us born again and offers us that chance through Him. Just realize what born again really means. Do not just try to add Jesus to other things in your life. Give your life fully to Him.

2. It is a gift. Now that phrase I just wrote ("Give your life fully to Him") sounds like a lot but realize it is God who is providing this opportunity for a new life to you. He did the work to make it happen. **2 Corinthians 5:18** says, "All this is from God." It is all from Him. He sees us getting what we deserve from our life choices but still wants to save us from the penalty of our sin. This is how much He cares and wishes to give us grace. God is rooting for us to be truly new in Him.

3. It is a process. While we can be changed positionally in God instantly (which is amazing and a blessing from God; see **John 3:16** and **Acts 16:31**), changing our life habits can take time. How does that change overwhelm us so we become new in practice as well as our position? **2 Corinthians 3:18** tells us how this happens. It starts with us beholding and looking at the "glory of the Lord." This means we are paying attention to God and focusing on Him. In other words, if we never open His word and if we never take time to meditate and think about the things of God, then we are never going to change. We need to observe Him, study Him, and think about Him, and then we start changing to become like Him. We are then able to be "transformed into the same image." As we constantly remind ourselves of how Jesus treated people, we start treating other people better. It is like a kid who really likes a TV character. He watches that show over and over and then starts talking like that guy on TV and acting like him. What happened? He saw this show, thought about this show when he was done watching, and became like that show. This verse tells us we do that with God. We see Him

and become more like Him. At some point, we will be able to look back at our life and see how far we have come.

So, like, this can really happen. I hope you want to be a new person. Every one of us needs to be changed in God and needs to keep changing. I need to see Him each day and to keep changing. So do you. Do not be the car that just has a new paint job and a new shine on the same old parts. Let God change who you are into something new. He wants to.

Day 63   Galatians 2:20

If ever you were looking for a life verse, this is one that could fit that description. **Galatians 2:20** is a verse that summarizes all of life for a follower of Christ in just one verse. Maybe today you are discouraged or maybe doing well. I don't know, but I do know that true life from this day forward can be found in this verse. So with an introduction like that, we better get into it.

1. "I have been crucified with Christ." Big statement. Crucifixion is a serious, permanent, painful death. Jesus went through it for me, so what does this mean? It means part of me died that day too—my sin died. My sinful old self died. The "me" who gets me in trouble, the "me" who speaks wrong things to me: that "me" died. This is sobering and beautiful all at once. It is beautiful because it means I can start anew in Christ. It is sobering because I need to not revive my old sinful self. Keep it dead!

2. "It is no longer I who live, but Christ who lives in me." Okay, so if my old sinful self does not need to live anymore, who am I? If I have given my heart to Jesus, then it is now Jesus who can live in me and through me. This "Who am I?" is a really important question in life. This verse is saying that I am someone different than I was before because Jesus has made a difference in my life. I have given my life to Him, and that gives me an amazing new identity—child of God (**John 1:12**). I no longer need to worry about eternity because I am loved by God. I no longer need to fight other people for status, recognition, or fame here on earth because I am loved by God. I do not need to live for wealth and stuff because I am loved by God. I can help others and love others because God has got my back. I am loved by God! It is no longer I who live—the "me" who needed to be the boss of my life and everyone else's life around me.

No, I can trust God and live for God because I am loved by God. It is Christ who lives in me.

3. "And the life I now live in the flesh I live by faith in the Son of God." God is giving me eternal life through His Son because of my faith in Him—faith alone, God's grace alone—but I still am living here on earth (living in the flesh) for a number of years. So how am I going to make it through this life? Answer: by faith in the Son of God. Since I am going to heaven, I have purpose in life here and now. Destiny determines purpose. I am destined to be with God, so why wouldn't I live for Him right now? But life right now is hard, and it can be discouraging. There are days that we are not sure we are going to make it. Everyone in our life is giving us a hard time, and nothing is working out like we thought it was going to. Faith. I have to have faith that God sees me (He does) and that He can take whatever is happening to me and use it for good (He can). I need to live this life trusting Him to take care of me. **Proverbs 3:5–6** says to put Him first, and he will direct our paths. He will. Too often, we panic and make bad decisions based on what we think we want or out of fear that life will turn bad for us. Following God and doing the next right thing will always turn out best in the end. Trust that God will turn your life circumstances to something good as He makes you into a better person for Him. You trust Him for eternity; trust Him for tomorrow. This is living faith.

4. "Who loved me and gave Himself for me." God is a loving father. He is! God could have looked at humanity and said, "They are broken" and just gotten rid of us, but instead, He loved us so much that He sent His Son to die for us and our sin. He loved us when we were sinners (**Romans 5:8**). Now if Jesus gave Himself for me, why would I live for anything or anyone else? I must remember every day the gospel message. This gives me peace that I am loved.

I do not know where you are at in your relationship with God, but I know that we all can be closer to him than we are today. Spend some time this week praying—open up your heart to God and ask forgiveness for your failures, commit your heart to Him more, tell Him your fears and worries, and tell Him to teach you more so he can lead your life. That is a prayer I need to do, as we all do. May God guide you in living this life in the flesh by faith in the Son of God who loves you and gave Himself for you.

Day 64   Romans 12 (Part 1)

Today we start a new series, and it is on a very practical chapter of the Bible, Romans 12. You are welcome to read the whole chapter, but today we will just look at the first two verses. I refer to these verses a lot as they are important guides to this life. We should all become familiar with **Romans 12:1–2**. Let's really break down these verses and look at them phrase by phrase.

1. Read verse 1. By using the word *brothers*, we see that Paul (the author of Romans) is talking to believers in Jesus who have already received the mercy of God through Jesus Christ. That is where we all begin—by receiving God's mercy and grace provided to us through Jesus. You see, Jesus was the final sacrifice for sin. There are no more sacrifices needed (**Hebrews 10:10–14**). So with that in mind, Paul then challenges us to be a new kind of sacrifice—a living sacrifice. We do not need to die for our sin; we get to live a new life. God says we can honor Him with our lives, and a life lived for Him is an acceptable sacrifice. It also mentions that this is our "spiritual worship." This means we are worshipping God when we are helping and loving others. Jesus said this Himself (**Matthew 25:34–40**), and this verse reminds us that if we have accepted Jesus, then it is time to live like Jesus.

2. But there is a force working against us in our effort to live a life of worship to God—it is this world that is around us. So verse 2 begins with the command to "not be conformed to this world." Conformed means to "be just like." Do not be just like the world—like everybody else. Our world looks like a party but is full of immorality, revenge, hatred, rejection of truth, and selfishness. Since we live in this world, it is very easy to follow these same messages. Remember, we get these messages all around us, especially

in media today, whether it be music, TV, videos, etc. For example, the movies and TV tell us these are no morals—just do whatever feels good. Then we in our lives start excusing some of our sins because we think everyone does it. What happened? We are becoming conformed to this broken world. **God wants us to change the world and not for us to be changed by the world.**

3. So what can we do about this influence the world has on us? We need to be "transformed by the renewal" of our minds. How does this happen? When we want to get in good shape physically, we watch what we eat and get healthy. It is the same thing spiritually. We need to feed on God more and more, whether that be by reading, listening, watching sermons, singing, being around God's people or however, but we need to feed our minds on more of God's thinking than the world's thinking. This is transforming and changing ourselves to be more like Jesus. It is a process for sure, but be patient and keep moving in God's direction.

4. Verse 2 says the end result of this renewal is that we can test what God's will is for us because God's will is good, acceptable, and perfect. The key word here is *discern*. We have to discern everything in life in order to *choose* what is best. Now, if I offered you a fresh cookie just baked or a stale cookie that sat on the table since yesterday, which would you choose to eat? The fresh one, of course! Good job discerning. But then, God offers us a peaceful and joyful life in Him, and we choose the stale activity of a party weekend instead because we have been conformed to the world and think this party is actually good for us. We need to be connected to God so we can make right choices that lead to a better life in God, which is what He wants for us. He wants what is best for us, and we need to be transforming and changing in our thinking in order to get there.

These two verses summarize how we can live life. It can be lived according to the sinful, broken world we live in, or it can be lived according to what God wanted for us all along. It all starts with what we feed our mind and thoughts on and goes from there. Take some time to think of some practical ways you can start transforming your thinking to be according to God. What habits can we make in our lives that will help us renew our mind and thoughts? You may be limited right now in what you can do, but that cannot be an excuse to not renew your mind starting today. We need to look at each day as an opportunity to get to know God a little better. We have to focus on God because the world is also knocking on our door each day. We are always conforming to something or someone. Why not conform to Jesus?

Day 65   Romans 12 (Part 2)

Last time, we started this important Bible chapter. Today let's read **Romans 12:3–8**. There is a lot in these verses, so we will pull out a few important points. Remember that these verses are written to people committed to following Jesus, and our goal is to not be conformed to this world but to be more and more like Jesus in how we live each day. These verses help us with that goal.

1. Pride. Verse 3 states that we should not think more highly of ourselves than we should. It says we should think with "sober judgment." What does this mean? Sober means to think clearly, and the verse wants us to be real with ourselves. Think about yourself and who you are. We have two tendencies here when thinking of ourselves—we either think we are nothing or we think we are all that. Here, Paul is telling the believers to remember their place—that the only reason we are anything is because of God and our faith in Him (now, if we think we are nothing, remember that God makes us something! But here, Paul is addressing the people that think too highly of themselves). Why do we think too highly of ourselves? The implication in verse 4 is that we look at others and compare ourselves—we can always find people that we think we are better than even within the Body of Christ (other Jesus followers). Stop it! This world likes making fun of others and looking down on others. No, we cannot be conformed to the world like that. A humble attitude accepts everybody and does not treat people as of less worth than me. The writer, Paul, realized he is who he is only because of the undeserved grace of God (**1 Corinthians 15:10**).

2. We are a team in Christ. Verses 4–5 emphasize that followers of Jesus look different from each other and have different abilities. This is by design so God can reach the differ-

ent people of the world through all of us. If someone does not have the personality that you do, that is okay; God can use that person in different ways. We all have different jobs in the kingdom of God. This is just like a sports team. In basketball, some players are big and play close to the basket, while others can dribble around the defense well, and still others can shoot, etc. In the same way, we followers of Jesus have different jobs within the common goal of reaching the world for Christ. This world really seeks to divide by our differences, but all that matters is Christ. Can you accept those who are different from you but also love Jesus? We need to appreciate those who are different from us.

3. Paul then lists a few of the jobs and gifts within the kingdom of God. We cannot all be teachers or preachers, but there are a couple jobs here that every one of us can do. Which are they from verses 6–8? I would specifically like to mention two of them: serving others and acts of mercy. All of us can serve others. All of us can do acts of mercy. An act of mercy is when I am kind to someone who does not deserve it. Mercy is helping someone I do not really know or I am not really friends with. I am merciful to that person because God loves him not because he deserves mercy. These acts of mercy are done because I have received mercy from God. Who am I to say you don't deserve mercy when I don't deserve mercy either! So we need to be looking for opportunities to do acts of mercy, as it says, with cheerfulness. It says that because we like giving people what they deserve—mercy is the opposite of that, and it is easy to grumble about the breaks someone else is getting. God sees you. It is okay. Give mercy.

4. I want to comment on one more area—leadership. It says to lead with zeal (lots of energy and excitement about leading). Look, many of you are leaders. People look up to you, and some of you have kids who look to you. Be a leader for Jesus. Be a leader who shows them the grace and mercy of God. When the world comes around you and closes you

in, follow **Romans 12:2** and be a leader in pushing back against this sinful world. You can lead by words of encouragement to others, and you can lead by example. Let's be honest, if you are reading this book, others in the block are noticing. They are looking to see what Jesus would do in situations—they will see that through you. Don't be a follower of this world and its thinking. Be a leader in showing others how it looks to live a life that is not perfect but is stepping toward Jesus a little bit more each day. May God give you strength to lead by example in a difficult place.

Day 66   Romans 12 (Part 3)

Hope you are hanging in there these days. Let's get back into Romans 12. The second half of this chapter (read **Romans 12:9–21**) is essentially describing for us what a follower of Jesus looks like. These commands are goals for us. We are still sinners and will not always make the mark, but this is an excellent passage for showing us practical areas we can improve on. Some of these areas, you will already be on top of, but others you will need to work on. We all have our different areas of strengths and temptations; we are all different people. Look for areas of weakness that you can emphasize in your life, and I will be doing the same for me. We all always need to be moving closer to Him in our lives.

1.   Genuine love. This will be a long list based on these verses over a few days. The first command in verse 9 is to have genuine love. What is love? What do you think? There are only a million songs out there describing love. Do most of those songs in pop culture describe genuine love? It seems like most of them describe a love that is more about doing what feels good tonight and not worrying about the future. How can that be true love? Hypocritical love is me showing love to you so that I get something from you in the end. We need genuine love in our life in order to show it to the world, and that kind of love only comes from God. In Luke 15 (yes, we are looking at that chapter again), Jesus tells a parable about a shepherd looking for a lost sheep (**Luke 15:1–7**). Hey, the sheep ain't lost—there were ninety-nine sheep to follow—he wandered off. This is its own fault. Just stay with the group. That sheep deserves to be lost, and yet the shepherd goes after it and rejoices in finding the lost sheep. We are that sheep that wandered off. God has no reason to search for us and accept us. But He does. We really offer Him nothing—we haven't worked up to deserve this

love—and yet He loves us anyway. That is genuine love. Jesus reemphasizes this kind of love later in the chapter with the parable of the prodigal son (**Luke 15:11–32**) who goes away and spends all his father's money—yet the father is ready to take him back. That son has nothing to give to his father except his wasted life—and still he is loved. That is genuine love. We need to understand that we are that prodigal son, and God's love to us is real. This changes our perspective on life and our future. Once we understand God's genuine love for us, we can show that genuine love to others, whether it is returned or not. We will have more on the practical side of love later in this chapter.

2. Hate evil. Hold on to the good (verse 9). This seems pretty easy to understand. Hate what is evil and what is bad for us and others. Hold on to what is good for us. What is the problem with this command? The problem is that we like what is evil! We like some things that aren't good for us. Why do we listen to that music/watch that stuff that isn't good for us? We like it. Why do we keep hanging out with those people that aren't good for us? We like it. Why do we keep going to that bar/club/place that isn't good for us? We like it. Why do we laze around all day and not work on our spiritual life (which is good for us!)? We don't like doing work—even spiritual work. Look, those are some bad sentences I just wrote, but I know that there is a part of me that likes being bad. That is my sin nature. It is there. I need to hate it. I know there is a part of me that wants to take shortcuts with God. I do not want to do the hard work of disciplining myself to get to know God better and actually help and show love to others. It is easier to do nothing. But that is what I need to hold on to. I need to remember how holding on to the good is hard work and is truly so much better for me. Each day, I need to choose to hate the evil that will draw me away from God and love what is good, which is God above all else. This is a battle. God wants me to win it. Each day, hate evil, love good.

We live in a world that will make excuses for evil. The world will tell us it is not that bad or that everybody's living this way. Doesn't matter. I need to hate the things that drag me down, even if I like them at first. The world will only show us the party; it isn't going to show us the aftermath and ruined lives that come later. God has given us a chapter like this so we can see what true living is like. We usually know the difference between good and evil. We just need to hate the evil rather than playing with it; and then love the good that comes from God.

Day 67　　　Romans 12 (Part 4)

Yesterday, we started going through the list of right ways to live listed in Romans 12. I appreciate that God helps us understand exactly what living for Jesus looks like. Read **Romans 12:9–13**. Today we continue our list in verse 10.

3. Love and honor. Notice what this verse is saying—*love* is a word that is sometimes thrown around loosely, so verse 10 clarifies to love with "brotherly affection." That is describing a deep care for others. Jesus always wanted His followers to love and care for each other (**John 13:35**). This world is full of selfish people; we don't need more of them. God is calling us to love others since He loves us. Think about ways you can do that and challenge yourself in that area.

The second part of this verse says to "outdo one another in showing honor." Do you realize how opposite of the world that thinking is? We live in a world where I need to look out for myself and put myself first to make sure I get the respect I deserve. I need to be honored! So many fights and disputes are started because we feel like someone disrespected us. We are quick to defend ourselves, but this verse is telling us to race to show honor to someone else. Outdoing each other in honor makes me think of two people about to go through a door and each of them saying, "After you." "No, after you." In life, we need to give honor to others without being concerned about what we get back in return. We have to allow ourselves to be honored by God and not worry about whether others respect us or not. That is a big statement, and others might not honor us, especially if we are seen as a Jesus-follower. But realize this is what Jesus is calling us to. We have to not worry about any honor we are not getting, like when Jesus was disrespected on the cross itself in **Luke 23:32–43**. May we focus more on respecting and honoring others than whether they are honoring us or not. God has got us so we can give and honor and love others.

4. Be fervent (zealous) in serving God (verse 11). What does this verse mean? Have you ever been really excited about an activity? Maybe you were going fishing or attending a sporting event, and all day you were just focused on the event to come and ready for it. We would say you were fervently waiting for the activity. You were zealous to do that. I can be zealous for a chance to play basketball. I find it fun and look forward to it. What about serving God? Do I have that same zealous or fervent spirit to do something for God? Hmmm. That is a different story. This verse says to not get lazy in zeal for the things of God. That is well said—we can get lazy and bored. Keep up your spirit for serving God. How is that done? Well, **2 Timothy 1:6–7** says to fan into flame what we have from God. How do you keep a fire going? Feed it. So we need to feed on the things of God. I know you are limited right now, but we do have technology to help us with Bible study or praise and worship or God's music or good and interesting preaching. We have books and the Bible. Keep all those things going in your life to feed the fire of zeal for God. Stay focused and fervent in serving Him while minimizing the distractions that the world has.

Look, this is hard work, and some days, let's face it, we don't feel very excited about spiritual things. But those are days where I need to push through. Sometimes, I do what is right simply because it is right. That's it. I know it is good for me. On other days, I can really feel the joy of the Lord in the midst of whatever circumstances. Please feed that fire for God. Do not let it go out. Seek encouragement from others who are on fire for God. Let those people be your friends and be a bright light for God. Please. In the end, serving God is best for you in your life, and it is best for others around you to see Him in you.

5. Hospitality (verse 13). I kind of went off on the last point and don't have space for verse 12 now, so let's skip to hospitality. This simply means to look out for each other, especially others who are also following Jesus. Help each other. Support each other. Encourage those who are also on this journey of life with God. We all need that kind of kindness from each other. If God blesses you with money or stuff, be generous in giving to God's work and charities. Help others in their times of need.

There is a lot here in these little phrases, and I am finding it a blessing to meditate on these verses this week. May God guide you as well.

Day 68   Romans 12 (Part 5)

We have been looking at Romans 12, and today we continue our list of practical ways to live like Jesus in **verse 12**. This is one verse with three related ideas in it:

6. (Continuing numbering the overall list from the previous days on Romans 12.) Hope, patience, prayer. These are three different phrases but are connected by tribulation. These are all tools we need in order to get through dark times in our lives. We all have hard times, and some of you have been through very deep difficult things in your life. I know that for some of you, right now is that dark and depressing time. How do we make it through these times? Life truly is a struggle, and if you are in Christ, sometimes life seems extra hard when you try to do the right thing. So what is the answer?

   - "Rejoice in hope." First, you need to focus on the future—far into the future of what we have in Christ after this life is over. This life is hard, but it will be over someday, and then we face eternity. Because of Jesus, we can rest in a sure future with God. Read these verses: **John 14:1–3, 2 Corinthians 4:16–18.** I just want to say again that this is a really important point. You can't make it through today if you are unsure of your tomorrow. Tomorrow for every one of us is eternity somewhere. God loves us so much He wants us with Him. He has done the work. You have to make the decision. Once you do, you are in God's hand forever. That fact is sometimes the only thing we have going for us in this hard life—but it is going for us. Make sure that you have accepted God's invitation to be on His team and in His hand. This is how we make it through today.

- "Be patient in tribulation." Being patient is never something we are excited about. We do not like to wait especially when waiting is hard to do. We can get very frustrated in times that are not going our way. God tells us to be patient in those times. Why are we in hard times (tribulation)? Maybe it was the result of our own bad choices; maybe it was because of someone else's bad choices, but let's be honest, it might be neither of those, and we may not know why we are going through a difficult time. We have to trust that God is in control and can guide us through these hard days. Remember your eternal hope and ask what you can learn from God at this time. In **Romans 5:1–5,** we are reminded that we might just need to learn some things through our hard times. Be aware of God trying to teach you something. He loves us and wants us all to be better.

- "Be constant in prayer." When life is easy for me, I tend not to spend so much time in prayer. This is a sad fact. I can forget God and fellowshipping with Him. On the other hand, when I am going through a crisis, I am pretty good at remembering to pray. This is how many of us work, sadly, and we need God to remind us to pray—which often happens through trials and problems. I wonder if sometimes we are forgetting God and He wants us to remember Him (for our own good!), so He allows some difficulty into our life. We tend to be more "constant in prayer" when we are in distress. The good news is that prayer is also what is going to help us make it through those hard times. Be faithful in sharing your heart with God. Open up and pray. Don't worry about saying the right words. God knows our hearts and just wants to hear from us—cry out to Him and ask Him to direct your life into His will. Be constant in prayer.

You might be going through some tough days right now, but I trust you are letting God speak into your heart. We need to be people that are open to whatever He wants to teach us. Give God some time each day. Allow yourself to have time to meditate and think on the things of God. Everything in life comes back to the one who gave us spiritual life as well as physical life. Encourage others in the things of God and show an example by being patient in tribulation. Uplift others and yourself in prayer.

Day 69   Romans 12 (Part 6)

Today, we continue in Romans 12. I trust you are finding your strength and encouragement in God. He is the one source of strength for our soul, who is always there for us because of Jesus Christ. Look to Him. Meanwhile, Romans 12 has been showing us practical ways to live out our life in God. And now we come to the tough stuff. I have been listing the characteristics in the second half of this chapter, and today we continue with number 7:

7.   (**Romans 12:14**) Bless those who persecute you

Okay, so is this for real? It literally tells us here to bless those who are persecuting us. Bless them? Return kindness to their insults? Yes, that is what it says. Hmmm. I would rather hit those who are causing me trouble, or I would rather go talk bad about them to others so everyone knows how bad they are. But this says to bless. This right here is a core teaching of Jesus. Everyone in the world can treat others the same way they treat us. That is easy. Jesus calls us to treat others better than they treat us. In **Matthew 5:16,** we are called to shine forth our good works to others. In **Matthew 5:38–42,** Jesus says we should not hit back. We do not need to have the last word in an argument. We can be the one who walks away without getting in the last insult. In **Matthew 5:43–48,** Jesus reminds us that our standard is God, not the world. Anyone can be kind to kind people. Followers of Jesus are amazing because we are kind to everyone, even jerks. Now a couple points about all this:

- If you are being harmed, it does not mean to stay in an abusive relationship. If people are leading you to do wrong, it does not mean to go along with them. We know this from other Scripture.
- It does mean we need to walk away sometimes rather than fight. This sounds like I am losing my honor, but I must

find my honor in God alone. In **Matthew 26:52–53,** we see Jesus saying He could call thousands of angels to fight for him, but that is not what He is all about. It is not about the fight, but it is about showing others how following Jesus can change your life.

- This all sounds like I am going to look weak. Yes, that might be true. But if we destroy others and cut them down physically or with our words, what will they think of Jesus? Ultimately Jesus is what will bring true peace, not pushing someone else into submission. Put other people into the hand of God and let Him deal with them (**Romans 12:19**)

8. Care for others' feelings (**Romans 12:15**)

This verse tells us to be happy with those who are happy and sad with the sad. Ultimately, this is telling us to care for the feelings of others. It means to empathize and sympathize with them—have compassion on them. Now, you might be reading this, thinking, *Chap knows we are men and not women.* Right? Yes, this is generally difficult for us men. Women are more in touch with their feelings, but we tend to just solve problems or tell others to "deal with it." This verse, though, reminds us to care for others and their feelings. I might not be going through what they are right now, but when people are hurting, they often need someone to talk with or to show them compassion. They need a dose of kindness, and that should come from us. If someone is happy, they want to share their story—you may not be in the mood, but listen for the sake of the other person. When someone is having a hard time, may we be the ones to go by and pray with them and for them. This is caring. This verse is telling us to be men who care.

The shortest verse in the Bible is **John 11:35**, which says "Jesus wept." His friend, Lazarus, had died, but Jesus knew he would come back. Yet Jesus still cried. Why? Because others were so sad, and He felt their pain. He was not so self-absorbed that He couldn't imagine what it was like to be someone else. A big way to be comforting to others is to put your arm around them and tell them you understand.

A big way to be encouraging to others is to be happy for them when something good happens rather than just thinking why it didn't happen to us. These verses are all about other people. Care for them. Love them. Show them through your attitude who Jesus is. May we be sure we are seeing Jesus each day in our hearts so we can represent him to others.

Day 70   Romans 12 (Part 7)

We have spent a week here in Romans 12 and still have some important practical points to cover. The lessons here for followers of Jesus are very practical, so that we have a clear picture of how we are supposed to live like Jesus. Let's start today by reading **Romans 12:16**.

9. Get along

This verse begins with the command to live in harmony, which is quite simply, to get along. How well do we get along with others in our life? In some ways, this is the most practical teaching in the Bible—I mean, we all want to get along with others. We don't like conflict that much (well, we do when we win, but that is another story), and life would be a lot easier if we got along with people. So this is a great command but leaves us with a follow-up question—HOW can we live in harmony and get along? That is the big question, isn't it? The good news is this verse also does guide us in how to do this. Here is what it says:

- No pride ("Do not be haughty"). I think we know how conflict starts. I have an argument with someone else because he thinks he is right about something—how could he think that when he should know that I am right! Yeah, so many arguments leave us insulting each other or simply trying to win an argument rather than trying to come to agreement (notice the difference). Why? Pride. We look out for ourselves a lot, and the Bible warns us so many times to be careful with pride. Here are just a few of the many verses on pride. Think about them. **Luke 22:24–27, James 4:6, 1 Corinthians 10:12, and Matthew 18:1–6**. Pride blinds us to our faults and causes us to not be growing and learning. Stay humble and teachable.

- Associate with the lowly. Read **Proverbs 17:5** and **Matthew 18:1–6** (again). This is true humility in action. Humility is realizing the value in other people, so seeing the value in "low" people is true humility and a key to getting along. Why? Because there are no low people in God's eyes. We look down on others because they are poor or act different from us. We want to hang with those who have money and can give us status and coolness (is that a word?). Jesus said to accept children. Random kids (Jesus just called a random kid in Matthew 18) do not give us anything of value—no money, no status, but we value them because they are precious human souls whom God loves. You know that guy you have a hard time getting along with? Just remember that he is also a precious human soul God loves. That does not mean you have to be best friends with everyone, but it does mean to value others because God values them.

- Do not be wise in your own eyes. Read **1 Corinthians 10:12** again. We always think we are right—if we didn't, we wouldn't do what we do. We always think we are right; we think we can do this and it won't harm us, we think we got life under control, and we think, *I got this*. Well, the problem is we don't always got this. Have you ever had that happen? I was so sure this would work out…whoops. This verse reminds us to be humble in our own attitude. Be careful so you do not fall. Now, that is the attitude we need to have so we can get along. If we all think we are right all the time, we will never truly get along since we all are doing our own thing. We will bully and plow over other people. It is good to be confident in life, but overconfidence is a killer. Be humble. Ask God for guidance. Respect others and listen to them too.

- **Romans 12:17**. Don't use someone else's evil and mistreatment of you as an excuse for you to mistreat someone else. This verse says to not repay evil for evil. We need to let it go to God. Let God take care of things for us rather than looking for revenge. Be the one who stops a feud by not hitting back or just let the other person have the last word. So what! God knows your heart, and that is what matters. We need more peace in this world, and we need to follow the pattern God has shown us here for it to happen. Going into today, may we be pushers of peace!

Day 71   Romans 12 (Part 8)

Today, we finish our study of Romans 12. Remember, when life is difficult for us, we can find our peace in God and in deeper under-standing of what Jesus did for us on the cross. God also calls us to be faithful even in hard times. May He give you strength. On to **Romans 12:18–20**.

10. In these three verses, we find one theme: do all you can to be at peace with others. So do you find this easy or hard to do? Let's look at the three thoughts:
    - Verse 18. "So far as it depends on you..." This means do <u>your</u> best to live at peace with others. Sometimes, others will not listen. You cannot control them; you can only control you. You make a point to do all you can to be at peace. That might mean apologizing for something that they do not forgive you for. That is sad, but you do your part. Be sincere and stay humble through the process.
    - Verse 19. No revenge. Pretty simple concept. The problem is that we start getting revenge on people from a very young age. Have you seen two-year-olds playing together? If one bonks the other on the head with a toy, what will the second one do? Hit back, of course. We kind of laugh at the two-year-olds, but fights like this aren't so funny once we are all grown-up. We say that we have to defend ourselves and show them who's boss, or we say, "Well, he started it." Maybe true, but all I know is what **Romans 12:19** says, and I know the world would be a more peaceful place if there wasn't revenge. Let God handle the other person. That is hard, but that is what this is saying.
    - Verse 20. Wait! This verse goes even one step farther! The idea here is when your enemy is doing bad to

you, you respond with kindness to him. This is heaping "burning coals" on him, or in other words will make him look bad (and hopefully realize his bad) by you returning goodness onto his badness! Think about that—Jesus is asking us to treat others way better than they treat us. This right here is like the hardest thing to do. If someone is rude to us, we want to smack him. If someone talks bad about me, well, now it is on. Jesus says to show them kindness even though they are treating you like their enemy. How can I do that? Really, the only way to do this is to remember that this is how God has treated me. I was an enemy of God. I want to rebel against the God of the universe and do my own thing. I fail Him, and He loves me anyway. I still fail God, and He still accepts me back. Hmmm. God is the one who does not treat me the way I treat Him. **Romans 5:8** says that Jesus died for me while I was a sinner. Wow. Do you want a second chance from God? How about another second chance with God after that one? And another? Yes, we do want second chances from God. And we get them. He then says, "Treat others like I am treating you." We need to give second chances and kindness to others, just like God gives to us. Read **Matthew 18:21–35**.

11. Fight evil with good (**verse 21**). Two statements are made in this verse.

   - One, fight the evil in your life. We all have it. Our sin nature is there. But we do not need to give in to it. Fight it. Do not give an inch. Evil wants to have you, but God gives us the strength to say no. Say NO. **Romans 6:17–18**.

   - Two, overcome the evil out there in this world with good. I think this means we should personally be treating others right, as we just said above, but also that we should be examples of goodness in this world.

Think about it. If we followers of Jesus do not care about people who are hurting or down and out, then why would the world want to learn about Jesus? If we can be the leaders of spreading goodness in this evil world and reaching out to hurting people, we can then truly overcome the evil in the world with good. God is good. Learn it from Him. Show it to the world.

This is a great practical chapter of the Bible. Romans 12 shows us what a follower of Jesus looks like. Remember, we are in a battle in this world as we saw in **Romans 12:1–2**. Each day, renew your mind and become a little more like Jesus. May God give us all the strength to stay true to Him.

Joseph is truly one of the most noble characters in the Bible who went through a lot and shows us many life lessons. We will take just a few days to see what we can learn from his life. His story begins in Genesis 37, but we will summarize and focus on chapters 39–41. You should read chapter 37 to see that Joseph is a teenager with ten older brothers who hate him. Joseph is trying to live right, but he is his father's favorite son, which doesn't go down well with his brothers, as you might expect. Eventually, the brothers sell Joseph into slavery to get rid of him and expect to never see him again. We pick up the story in Genesis 39 with Joseph in Egypt as a slave. Read **Genesis 39:1–20**.

The Story: Joseph is sold to a prominent family in Egypt, and he decides to work hard in this bad situation. Unfortunately for him, he is a handsome guy; the wife notices and trouble ensues. Joseph, of course, is wrongly accused in the matter and winds up in prison. That is not exactly the reward he was looking for when he chose to honor God and not this woman. But life is not always fair, even for (especially for?) those who choose to do what is right.

Lesson 1: Work for God, not for men.

Imagine what it was like for Joseph to be betrayed by his brothers. Wow. Now he was in a strange country and is forced into slavery. He is not excited about his new life, as we will see next lesson, but still, he decides to work hard for this Egyptian guy anyway. He works so hard and is so responsible that he is promoted to chief of staff for the household. Why would he work that hard in such a bad situation like that? Why wouldn't he just do the minimum effort to survive and try to escape? Answer—Joseph was working for God and not for men. Read **Colossians 3:23–24**. We do not do work for men but for God. We are now members of God's kingdom, and that changes things. Maybe we would take little shortcuts before or even be tempted to be dishonest at work. Not anymore. We work for God, whatever our job is.

Lesson 2: Run from sexual temptation.

Have you ever made a bad choice with a woman? Have you ever played around with some girl, and then it ended badly? We have to learn from Joseph. Look, he was in the perfect situation—this woman was in charge of the house—her husband was out all day long every day. Joseph totally could have gotten away with an affair with her, or even just a few good times. As a matter of fact, the last time she came to him, they were the only ones in the house—no other servants or anyone. Notice how Joseph answered her: "How then can I do this great wickedness and sin against God?" Joseph was not even thinking about his relationship with Potiphar, her husband; Joseph was thinking about his relationship with God. Sometimes we do sin against other people, but every sin is against God and will affect our relationship with Him. Joseph realized this and would not break. God meant more to him than what she could offer.

But do you also see how Joseph dealt with this temptation? There are some sins that we need to stand and fight against. This is not one of them. We need to run from this type of temptation. **2 Timothy 2:22** says to "flee youthful passions." Flee! Joseph ran because this is not a temptation to stand there and think about. Remember David when he saw beautiful Bathsheba? David looked, thought, and a way to sin opened up. Not Joseph. He realized this is not a good place to be and got out. Notice also that no one else was in the house. This was trouble and opened up the lie that would put Joseph in jail. Don't be alone in a house with a woman who is not your wife—that is a sure way to avoid trouble and avoid accusations.

We, as men, need to be careful in relationships with women. If you are married, you cannot have girlfriends, physically or emotionally. If you are single, don't get involved in a physical relationship until after you are married. This is what God says is best, because it is. These days, this type of temptation is easy to play with—it comes to us on our phones. Safeguard your life and protect yourself. Joseph did all he could do. So should we. We need to be men who are leaders in honorable relationships with women. Here are a few more important verses to read on this topic. May God guide you. **Job 31:1, Proverbs 4:23, 1 Thessalonians 4:3–8, and Proverbs chapter 7.**

Day 73   Joseph (Part 2)   Genesis 39–41

When we last saw Joseph, he had taken a stand against temptation and made the right choice before God. His wonderful reward for doing what was right was being sent to prison. So this would be an excellent opportunity for Joseph to get angry with God and tap out of his relationship with Him. But read **Genesis 39:20–23**. What happened? Was Joseph forgotten by God? No. Did Joseph take the job that he had in prison and do it for God's glory? Yes. That is something else, really. He was betrayed by his brothers, faithful to God, rewarded with prison for it, and still lived his life for God wherever he was. He realized God was with him. He knew God was in control. That is hard, but Joseph kept doing what was right. What stops us from doing right? Being wrongly accused? That didn't stop Joseph. Being in a terrible place? That didn't stop Joseph. Living for God happens all the time wherever we are. Now, did Joseph have some supernatural power to not feel bad when these things happened? No—let's see how he actually felt about all that was going on in his life.

Read **Genesis chapter 40**. Take a moment to review what happened. Joseph is in prison, and two guys from the Pharaoh's court come and have dreams that disturb them. Joseph has acknowledged God in his life and says God can help give the interpretations (v. 8). The first guy (cupbearer) gets a positive meaning—you will get your job back! The second guy is pretty excited but finds out his dream means he will lose his job, and his head. Joseph is very interested in the cupbearer. He now knows a guy who works directly with the Pharaoh. This guy knows people! This guy can help get Joseph out of here! So Joseph tells him his story in verses **14–15**. Notice that Joseph says that he was stolen out of his homeland (in other words, taken away by slave traders) and had done nothing to deserve prison (falsely accused). Joseph was not excited about being in prison. He wanted out. I mention this because in verses like this, we see that Joseph was like us. He was upset. He was looking for any chance to get out and live his life again. He was not superhuman. He was very human. But that makes his decisions to do what was right even more impressive. He was not happy with being where he was, but he was going to honor God anyway.

And that brings us to the last verse in this chapter. What does it say? The cupbearer forgot Joseph. He did not remember him. Now look at **chapter 41 verse 1**. Two years pass by. This had to be the worst time ever for Joseph. He knew the cupbearer was out and had an influential position. Joseph thought this guy was coming to get him out any day now. Can you imagine being Joseph—every day he would hear the prison door open and quickly run to the door hoping to see his friend there to take him out, and it wasn't. Well, maybe tomorrow. The door opens again, and again, nothing. Nobody for Joseph. He had that expectation for weeks and months and then two years. Nothing. This had to be the worst. Now, it wasn't just that he was wrongly there but that every day he had hope that failed. Wow.

At this point, we could understand Joseph being angry and leaving God. We can understand Joseph saying forget it and not working hard in the prison anymore. Remember, he had been given a job of responsibility there—but what was the point? The cupbearer forgot him. God forgot him. Or did He? You see, this is where faith really comes into play. Anyone can have faith and trust that God sees him in the good times, but true faith is needed in the bad times. I am sure it was incredibly hard for Joseph, but he stayed faithful. Discouraged, but faithful.

We have to remember that God is working on a much longer timeline than us. We want things now. We want everything to work out immediately, but God is looking at the big picture of our life and wants to teach and develop us. That takes patience and faith on our part. We have got to trust that God can take our worst situations and use them for Him. Job was an example of suffering for God but had to trust God in the dark. **Job 23:8–10** are amazing verses. Job admits in verses 8–9 that he cannot see God. Job does not see what God is doing. Yet he still says verse 10—I know he is seeing the way I take. Job wants to win the race of life, and in his hardship, he says I will come out as gold. Wow. Life is hard. I won't say it is easy. But we have to trust that God sees us (He does), and that we can come out of this all as gold. Be strong in trusting in who God is. He has got you, even when you don't see it.

Day 74   Joseph (Part 3)   Genesis 41–50

I could write a lot more on Joseph's life, but I am just going to summarize the remaining chapters of Genesis and look at two big lessons we can see from the rest of Joseph's life. When we left off, Joseph was greatly discouraged having been forgotten in prison, but two years later, he was seen. You can read **Genesis 41** to see how Joseph was brought out and up to serve right under Pharaoh, the leader of Egypt. Happy ending, except he still had to deal with his past, and that happened when his brothers came to him in **Genesis 42–44**. In those chapters, we see that Joseph did not seek revenge, but he did test them to see if they had changed. It culminates in an emotional reunion in **Genesis 45:1–15**.

Here we see the first lesson from this part of the story. We must forgive. Jesus talked about forgiveness a lot. But we also see that "forgiveness is given now, but trust is earned over time" (see Day 59). Joseph forgave his brothers and did not get revenge on them, even though he could have done whatever he wanted with them. That is for God to decide, not us. On other days, I have mentioned how we must remember that God has forgiven us of so much that we must show forgiveness to others. But that does not mean we should rush back into an unsafe relationship. That is where Joseph was. He had to see if his brothers cared about Benjamin, who was the youngest brother. Could he trust them? In this case, much time had passed, and they were changed people. That is not always the case, and even though we forgive, it may not be a good idea to have the same relationship with someone, at least not at first. For example, if someone borrows money from me but doesn't pay me back, I can forgive him and forgive the debt, but I am also not ready to let him borrow more money until he can prove to be trusted. This is a hard one emotionally because we all need forgiveness and second chances. We just need a lot of wisdom with some people in our lives because we cannot rush back into an abusive or harmful relationship. Distance is needed sometimes. Joseph had the advantage of a lot of time passing and got to see that they did care for each brother, unlike before. Again, we need God's deep wisdom in this area.

Well, Joseph is reunited with his father (**Gen 46:28–30**), and the story continues on happily until Joseph's father gets old and dies. At this moment, the brothers are scared that Joseph did not kill them only for the sake of their father, and they are in trouble now. Joseph says an amazing verse at this time, though. Read **Genesis 50:15–21**. In verse 20, Joseph says, "God meant it for good." At the end of everything, he saw that God had been at work earlier when he could not see Him. God took what was evil and turned it around to use it for good. That is our second lesson.

God can take all things and turn them to good for our learning and for our growing in Him. You know when we need that lesson, right? We need it when we are like Joseph—hopeless in the prison or in life. Joseph must have had this idea with him because what did he do when life got bad for him? He stayed faithful to God and did his work for God—his work as a slave and his work as an inmate. Not fun. Discouraging. He did not know if he was getting out of prison and knew he did not deserve to be there. When there is nothing else to do, we have to remember God. We have to stay faithful—stay faithful when it is hard to stay true to God. Stay true when we don't know the end of the story.

I do not know how you are doing today, but God has given us this verse, **Genesis 50:20**, for bad times. I have to know and believe that God can turn our misery into good. Read **Romans 8:28–29**. The lesson there is not that life turns out perfect, but that God is working for our good—and good is to be like Jesus. Joseph grew in maturity and strength in God through these difficult years. He did not have to stay faithful to God when he felt abandoned. But he did. And God used it for good. If you are going through hard times right now, I do not know how it will turn out, and I can't tell you everything will be great in the end. I can tell you that God has not forgotten you and wants you to be close to Him in your life. We can always look to God. We can always remember Him and talk to Him and trust that he is there. Joseph was frustrated but did this. Years later, he was able to say God meant it for good. I hope years from now, you can also say that whatever happens, this time was the turning point for you in your relationship with God.

Day 75 **Not Hopeless (Part 1)** John 4

Today we start a new little series. Do you ever feel like you have lost all hope? You have tried life and life failed you? Jesus came so that we would have life and have it abundantly—so we could have a life (**John 10:10**). Do not lose hope. But you must look to Jesus. I want to see a few people in God's word who were pretty hopeless but then found Jesus. Today is a story that is familiar to us, but the Samaritan woman's story is so important to us in understanding our hope in Christ. Read **John 4:1–42**.

We need to understand the life of this lady. It says that Jesus was traveling and met her at the well at the sixth hour. This is the sixth hour of daylight in the Middle East—that means noontime in a very hot climate. No wonder Jesus was tired. But why was this woman at the well at the hottest part of the day? And where was everyone else? No one would want to gather their daily water in pots at noon—even today in small villages without running water, people gather their water in pots at sunrise and right before sunset. That explains why no one else was there, but why was she there? Ummm, she said she had five husbands and was with a guy now who was not her husband. She was a loose woman. She slept with a bunch of guys. And the village did not like her. In that culture where the family unit was so strong, a woman like that was despised and looked down on. And for good reason! Even today, watch out for that woman who is willing to sleep with every guy in town. But what about her?

So she had no friends. She clearly had no family of her own. Maybe she had lost them or been rejected by them. But why was she sleeping around? She was searching for acceptance in the arms of different men. People do that today too, right? Some women and some men search for "love" but are really looking for acceptance. People have disappointed us, and we are hoping the next relationship is just a little bit better. But it usually isn't. This woman was tired. She was tired of failed relationships, and she was tired of carrying water at the hottest time of day! In verse 15, she jumped at the thought of not coming to the well again. She probably hated her life: no peace, empty relationships, rejection, and a lot of hard work just to get some water. She is hopeless.

Now, she has some knowledge of religion, but she is chasing the wrong ideas there too. She is focused on what she needs to DO. Do I worship here or do I have to go to Jerusalem to find God? She is focused on works—and if finding God happens through works, she better get busy because she has a lot of sin to make up for! But Jesus says something different to her. He says it isn't about what you do or where you do it. It is about your heart—it is about worshipping God through the Messiah—through the One who came from God. It does not matter where you are. You need Jesus. Jesus came to make up for all those sins and years of chasing spiritual water in wrong worship, wrong works, and a wrong lifestyle. She needed the true and living water. This water is a gift, and you will never be thirsty again. You see it? She was chasing satisfaction in men and in spiritual rules/works. Neither left her satisfied because we can only find true spiritual peace in Jesus Christ and what He is offering to us.

So what happened? She believed. She accepted what Jesus was offering—that new life in Him. What about her sin with men? In the past. What about her rejection by the village? This is interesting because instead of getting revenge on her village for rejecting her, she went and told them all about Jesus. She brought them to Him. She understood forgiveness. She was forgiven of her sin, and she could be free to forgive her village. She was excited. She had found hope. True hope and true meaning for life.

Yeah, it really is quite a story. What have you been chasing in this life? What have you been trying in this life? The best answer is the same answer that woman found. Jesus. True forgiveness. We worship Him in spirit and in truth—good thing because our works don't cut it. He knows. Rest in God's forgiveness and go forward in God's forgiveness like this woman did. And one other thing. We are always excited to share with others good news. If there was free ice cream, we would tell others where to get it. There is free living water in Jesus. Let's be like the woman who was excited to talk about that! Because no one is hopeless in Him. Stop chasing what doesn't work. Accept the living water of Jesus.

Day 76   **Not Hopeless (Part 2)**   Luke 5

How helpless have you ever felt? Maybe you have felt so beyond help that you became just hopeless. Today we will see a guy who was in a pretty hopeless situation until he met Jesus. Read **Luke 5:17–26**.

We have the story today of a guy who couldn't walk. Can you imagine living two thousand years ago with no technology and not being able to move around? That would be hard. This guy was living a hard life. But then, there was some good news—his friends heard about Jesus who had been healing some people. Wow. Now this guy had a little hope. Maybe he would walk again. Maybe. But then, they arrive at the house, and it is already crowded. He can't get in until his friends raise the roof for him! He gets sent right to the presence of Jesus. Wow. This is the moment of hope. This is the moment it all can happen—he will be able to walk. And Jesus says, "Your sins are forgiven."

Wait a minute. I thought the guy was going to be able to walk. How do you think he felt right now? Probably disappointed about his lack of walking. Was he excited about forgiveness of sin? I don't know, but he should have been. You see, he thought he needed physical healing, but Jesus knew it was more important for him to have spiritual healing. There is a lesson in there, right? We are pretty focused on the physical and how much we need in this life, but Jesus knows how much we need true spiritual help above all else. What good is making it in this life if we are not ready for the next? Read **Luke 12:13–21**. We cannot be so focused on getting ahead in this life that we forget the next life.

But wait, this guy still needed to eat. He still needed physical healing, and it was all a test of faith for him because he had to believe Jesus's words about forgiveness of sin. The good news is Jesus gave him more reason to believe he was forgiven by healing his walking problem. And he rose and walked.

So let's think about all this for a minute and how it applies to us:

1. First things first.

We all have many needs. Our physical needs are big needs. Very big. You may not have a support system or place to go from here or a future job. Those need to be addressed. But you have got to be right with God first. He will guide your future. But you've got to let Him guide you. This man needed to walk. But he needed to be good with God first. Some people say they will give God more time once they get their feet under them and get settled. Wrong order. God has to be first, and He will help you get settled.

2. You are not alone.

This guy could not even walk to Jesus. He needed others to carry him. But those guys showed up and got him to Jesus. I do not know who God will bring along your path, but He can do it, and He can help you. You are not hopelessly alone. There are groups of believers out there that want to help you. Let God help you, and let God's people help you. This man did. It turned out well for him.

3. What you need may not be what you think you need.

This guy thought he was hopeless physically. The reality was he was hopeless spiritually and needed a Savior. He found Him. God knows what you need. This story is similar to **John 9**. That whole chapter is the story of a blind man who was thrilled to see, but maybe realized at the end that what he really needed was a Savior. He found that Savior even as he was losing his family, but he rejoiced in God coming to him. I encourage you to read that chapter and also realize that God knows what you need. Trust Him.

4. Be the friend.

A lot of this lesson has been focused on ourselves, but now let's focus on others for a minute. This guy who got healed in Luke 5 needed some friends to carry him. Can you be that friend? Can you be that friend to someone who is feeling hopeless? A lot of people might not admit it but are feeling pretty depressed here. What can you do to help show others there is hope in Jesus? I do not know the answer to that question, but I know there is an answer. God wants to use you to encourage others. We have a world that is broken, and we know the true answer to brokenness. Help others see a little hope.

Conclusion of this story? Get to Jesus. He knows what we need. Stay close to God so He can guide you both now and on the outside. He is our true hope.

Day 77   **Not Hopeless (Part 3)**   Luke 19

Today, we look at a guy who did not think he was hopeless for most of his life. He had all he ever wanted. He lived a good life until he realized pouring your life into money is actually pretty worthless in the end. Read **Luke 19:1–10** for the story of Zacchaeus (we will call him Zac from now on, agreed?).

For some of you, this is a familiar Bible story of a short guy who climbed a tree to see Jesus. But let's think for a minute about what these verses tell us. He was short. I'll bet he figured out early on in life that basketball was not in his future. He also was not going to physically fight his way to the top. So I'll bet when he was young, he was picked on for his size, and he determined to get back at everyone. And he studied numbers. And got a job in finance. He became a tax collector. And he was good at it. He got so many promotions that he became "a chief tax collector" (verse 2). And so he won. He was rich. Not only that, but as a tax collector, he could take advantage of his position and cheat people out of even more money. That will teach them for making fun of his shortness! He would have the last laugh for sure.

So Zac did it. He had all he wanted. But then he realized a few things. While he had the money, a lot of people hated him. So he had new friends. Bad friends—"sinners." Maybe he also lost some of his joy. I mean, you can only buy so many Roman souvenirs and trinkets. Somewhere around this time, he heard about this guy Jesus. Jesus was supposed to be something else—a Savior actually. Zac started realizing his life needed some saving. Money was not the answer to what really matters in life. Maybe he even started feeling a bit hopeless. Until he heard Jesus was coming to his town! So Zac rushed downtown, but the crowds were too many, and he was too short. He had an idea—and he ran ahead to climb up a tree. He would be able to see Jesus from there. And he did! Jesus actually walked over to his tree! And invited Himself over Zac's house for lunch! Zac was overwhelmed. He was amazed. He was also humbled. People were asking why Jesus would go to a house of a sinner, but Zac did not care what they said—besides, they were right. He was a sinner. But Jesus was offering Zac a new life, and he was serious about following Jesus. How could he prove to the people that he was serious about this Jesus following thing? Zac got an idea and could hardly believe his own ears when he heard himself saying, "The half of my goods, I give to the poor." Not only that, but Zac said he would pay back four times the money from anyone he cheated.

What a change! Why? Because Zac realized it is hopeless to follow money. We all think money will buy us happiness and peace. It doesn't. Wealth is actually pretty deceitful—it tricks us into thinking we are good. It tricks us into giving our lives over to money and doing anything for it. Anything. We are hopelessly deceived by wealth. Zac knew he needed to give it away. He would control money. Money would not control him. Read **1 Timothy 6:6–10**. Read those verses carefully. Sometimes, the most hopeless people have put all their hope in the riches of this world.

We all live for something, but only one thing really matters—preparing for life after this world. A life apart from Jesus cannot bring that true hope. Now, here is some really good news. Jesus came to help hopeless people. Did you see what happened in the story? Jesus looked for Zac and went over his house. What did the other people say—the "religious people"? They were upset that Jesus went there. They knew who Zac was and who his friends were—they were known sinners. But Jesus did not run away from the sinners; He actually went to them. Then he defended His actions by telling His main purpose in coming here to earth—He specifically came to "seek and to save the lost." See what He said—SEEK. Jesus is looking for people He can help. Jesus is looking for those who are hopeless and wants to save them. Stop and think about that a minute. He is looking for the hopeless.

So where are you at? What are you living for? Finding your value in wealth? Hoping to have enough money to not worry about money? Yeah, that would be nice, but it is also empty. Jesus came to fill that empty spot. People matter. God matters. Zac had a hole in his heart that he thought he could fill with money. Nope. God needs to fill it. What holes are in your life? God wants to fill them—He is even looking for you—He is seeking out the lost so He can save them. That sounds like no one is beyond hope. No one is actually hopeless.

Day 78   **Not Hopeless (Part 4)**   John 3

We are continuing to look at some people in the Bible who were hopeless until they weren't, because they met Jesus. To start today, read **Luke 18:9–14**.

When you read that, who do we first suspect is the hopeless one? The tax collector, right? That guy must have been a cheat of some sort and even called himself a sinner, while the Pharisee was a keeper of the law. He was noble, and, of course, thought that he was all that. But Jesus is teaching here that those who humble themselves before God are not hopeless. They are accepted! It is the ones who do *not* humble themselves—the ones who think they got it together who are in trouble.

So some of us might realize who we truly are and humble ourselves before God, but let's face it, a lot of the time we are like that Pharisee. Think about it—what was the last thing you said before you fell spiritually, morally, or physically? "I got this," right? We always think, "I got this," when we don't. Even when we are right with God, we start making our own plans for the future and maybe make some questionable decisions. We say things like, "I can handle it," and "But he is my friend," and "I will be able to tell them I won't join them," and "I know what she is like, but it is a free apartment." These are not the words of someone who is humbly following God. Those are the words of someone who is like that Pharisee and thinks they got their life under control. No, that person is actually hopeless. That is Jesus's point from these verses. He wants to grab the attention of some people who think they got it all together.

Okay, well, what about that Pharisee? What does that guy need to do in order to not be hopeless? I think number one is realize he is hopeless. When we are relying only on ourselves, we are absolutely hopeless even if we don't realize it (read **1 Corinthians 10:12**). Now, this is a slow realization, and a hard one. We do not want to admit we can't do it. But that is exactly why we are hopeless. The answer is to go to Jesus. That is what a different Pharisee did in John 3. Read **John 3:1–21**.

Nicodemus was a Pharisee. Why was he coming to talk with Jesus at night? Peer pressure. Among those who are Pharisees and got it all together, how could Nicodemus admit that he did not know all the answers? He couldn't, so he came to Jesus at night. He learns about this "born again" thing. Those two words say a very big message. Jesus did not say to Nic, "You are pretty close to me as a good Pharisee. You don't need much fixing, maybe just a little change here and there, but you are pretty much ready for the kingdom of God." No, being born again is a complete change. Being born again is a complete renewal that gets rid of our old self, our old being. Jesus knows we need complete change, and those who think they don't need complete renewal are fooling themselves and are hopeless, whether they realize it or not. Isn't that what Jesus is saying in verse 10 when he says Nic is a teacher in the land—how does he not know these things? He doesn't know because he has spent his life as a Pharisee thinking he is better than other people and is doing fine. He is blind to God's love (verse 16).

There is one other implication here in verse 19. Some people finally understand that their life does not match up to God, but they like the darkness anyway and don't change. They don't accept the light of Jesus because it would require too much change. The fact is that sometimes we like what we do. Sin gets hold of us, and we don't really down deep want to leave it. We are hopeless.

Where are you at today? Again, at first, I don't think we would admit we are like the Pharisee in the first story, but the main point of a Pharisee is that he doesn't need any help. He has got this. He is better than others around him anyway, so he thinks he is okay. Wow. What that Pharisee really needs is to be born again. He needs a full change of life. Now are you ready to let God really change you? Not just a little change, like you saying, "When I get out, I will try to go to church," which really means you will think about getting closer to God once or twice but will not make any deep changes. What would Jesus say? He would say you need to be totally new and reborn in Him. Your life is not hopeless, but it is if you think you are okay.

Jesus told us that (read **Matthew 16:24–26** right now). We need to humbly come before Him and give all of our heart to Him. It is for our own good.

Day 79   **Not Hopeless (Part 5)**   Acts 8

Today is the last day in this series, and I want to start off with a Bible story. Read **Acts 8:26–40**.

Here is this guy, an Ethiopian eunuch, which means he had some government job which was pretty important, as it says. His status as a eunuch meant he could be trusted around the queen (not the way I would want to get a job, but whatever). He apparently was on a search for God. He heard about lots of worshippers in Jerusalem, had gone there, and was reading some of the Old Testament. He was actually reading from **Isaiah 53** which is a moving chapter describing the death of Christ for our sins. The Ethiopian is a bit confused about whom these verses are talking about, but God sends Philip along to explain. The man is excited, believes, is baptized, and the rest is history. (Actually, it is history because it is interesting to note that there has been a Christian presence in Ethiopia for centuries since that time. You can see how God used this man's influence with the queen to spread the Good News to the people of that land.)

Now think about this man. He was pretty hopeless. How was he ever going to learn about Jesus? The answer is that God sent along two things—His word and His man. The Ethiopian had God's word, which made him curious about God's truth. And then right when he needed it, God sent along a person, Philip, to explain. You realize that we also are not hopeless in these areas today either? We have these things. You have God's word right here in prison, where we are. God has people ready to explain His word in your life. Look, the gift of God's word is a beautiful thing. We can just sit and read God's message to us. That is an amazing privilege. Read God's word. Read it slowly for understanding. Ask questions.

There is a group of people also in Acts who did this. Read **Acts 17:10–12**. Here is a group of people who were eager to receive the word of God and daily examined the word. Daily. Daily is important. We need to renew our minds and keep our minds in God each day. Examined. This means it wasn't just a quick skimming that did not sink in. No, this was a deep reading with brains engaged. If you got a love letter from someone, how would you read it? Slowly, carefully, trying to think about every word. This is God's love letter to us! He cared enough to tell us about Himself and how we can easily come to Him. We are never hopeless if we are in God's word.

But what next? We have to do it. Read **Matthew 7:24–27**. Jesus has just finished preaching, and everyone is feeling pretty amazed, and also pretty good because they have just heard such words of wisdom. But what will they do with it? What will you do with what you hear from God? This is really important because there are many men who have come through prison, turned to God during their time in here, but forgotten Him as soon as they get on the outside again. What happened? The word of God is good, but it is we who take shortcuts. We don't make time for God. We are faced with serious changes in our lives if we are going to follow God's word. We have to make those changes. The difference between a hopeless life and a hopeful life in God is God. You will be hopeful if you allow God to be big in your life, but you will become hopeless in whatever else you are living for if it is not God.

Overall, with this series, I want to encourage you in God. I want you to see the way to true hope. It ultimately comes from resting in who God is and His love for you. You are not too far from hope. I was reading a book last week called *Gentle and Lowly*. The author said this: "The same Christ who wept at the tomb of Lazarus weeps with us in our lonely despair. The same one who reached out and touched lepers puts his arm around us today when we feel misunderstood and sidelined. The Jesus who reached out and cleaned messy sinners reaches into our souls and answers our half-hearted plea for mercy with the mighty invincible cleansing of one who cannot bear to do otherwise."[2]

That is the deep love of God for us through Jesus Christ. We are not hopeless. Nope, we are more than conquerors through Him who loved us (**Romans 8:37**). Get to know Him better daily. Spend time with Him. Read his letter to you. Be strong in the hope that stays. May God guide that walk you have with Him.

---

[2] Ortlund, Dane. *Gentle and Lowly* (Crossway: Wheaton, Illinois, 2020), page 32.

Day 80   **Hebrews 12:1–2**

Today we see a couple famous verses which are great motivational words for our lives. We all need to keep these words in front of us as we go forward in life. Take a moment to read **Hebrews 12:1–2**. This is about running the race of life—do you ever feel like life is a race and others are passing you by? I think we all have times when it is just hard to be pumped up about this race of life, but we really need to fight against discouragement and stay focused on living this life for God—the true reason to live. Hebrews 12:1–2 gives us guidelines on how to do that—specifically five ways:

1. You are not alone. The phrase "surrounded by so great a cloud of witnesses" refers back to Hebrews 11 and all the believers who came before us and were found faithful. This phrase tells us to look and see that we are surrounded by others who did life and made it. They went through hard times, but God was still with them. God used them to do great things. Find mentors who love God—those who have turned it around in Him. Make friends with those people now and remember God's people of the past.

2. Lay aside every weight. This phrase reminds us that runners do not run carrying backpacks! They wear light clothing that does not weigh them down so they can run faster. What are some weights in your life? They may not even be sin—they are just distractions that keep us from growing in Christ and being fully committed to Him. We all carry different weights—maybe issues from our past (see point 5 below) or bad habits now. Put them aside. Drop them. Give your weights to God and run the race without carrying burdens. Jesus went to the cross to set us free. Don't go back

3. Speaking of going back, it also says to drop the sin which "clings so closely" to us. That is true. Sin really sticks to us,

and we need to get out from under its power. Too often, once we start down a road of sin, it only becomes easier to repeat that sin (read **Romans 6:16**). Address those sin issues in your life and commit them to God. Each day, make the next right choice. Every day you do this is a victory. All those victorious days will add up to a life. Now read **Romans 6:12–14**. We have to find our victory in Christ and give ourselves to Him—recommit to Him each day.

4. Run with endurance. We need to live life ready to endure. I have worked with teenagers a lot in my life, and teens really tend to live for the moment. Many times in schools where I taught, I would have conversations with teens that involved the question, "What were you thinking?" Usually the answer was "I wasn't thinking." Now, we all have some of that "live for the moment without thinking" attitude in us, but that does not prepare us for the long haul. We need to look at our life as a long journey or race and prepare accordingly. Living for the moment is an excuse for sin and lack of preparation for the future. A runner will not show up for a race after sitting on his couch for the previous two months. He will train every day, even if he does not see results daily. He knows the discipline of training is working for the greater good. It is the same with us if we can just remember Christ and focus on becoming a little more like Jesus every day.

5. Which does bring us to the conclusion—for all this to work, we have to look to Jesus. He is what we are looking at, just like a runner looks forward in a race. This means a few things:

    a) No looking back. We cannot go through life looking backward—a runner would never do that! We cannot let yesterday's failures hold us down or yesterday's successes make us relax. Read **Philippians 3:13–14** and **1 Corinthians 10:12**. No dwelling on the past—Jesus came so we did not have to be tied to our past.

b) To live is Jesus. He already endured suffering and shame for us. He did not give up but endured. Life will be hard, for sure. If we live for God, there will be people who are against us and try to discourage us. Read **Hebrews 12:3**, the next verse. Jesus endured the hostility of sinners. Of course, we will too. That is why we have to have our life dominated by the purpose of living for Him. Sinners will not be happy with us if we choose to follow Jesus rather than sin since, as I like to say, "nothing makes a bad activity look good like having a lot of people do it." But it is still sin and is still what is bad for us. Look to Jesus and endure suffering that will come from the world because we are not living for this world. We are living for Him, the one who loves us and saved us. Be strong in Christ.

Have you ever been called for something? Think back to when you were in school. Do you remember sitting there in class not really paying attention (or paying too much attention to who you were sitting next to!) when, all of a sudden, the teacher called your name? Teacher asked you a question, and not only did you not know the answer, you didn't even know the question! But wait, maybe there was another time you were called. Perhaps it was to act in a play or join a sports team at recess or even for the official school team. In that case, you were really hoping to get called. Maybe you had that experience of getting called in a good way…or maybe not. Maybe you were never called to anything good. I do not want to bring up bad memories, but listen, I have some very good news for you. Read **Romans 1:1–6**.

In this introduction to the book of Romans, Paul writes about how Jesus is everything. Jesus was talked about in old times and showed that He was truly the "Son of God in power" by rising from the dead. Paul says that he has received grace from God through Jesus because he had the "obedience of faith." That is a big statement from Paul because he was a big sinner. His sin was physically attacking those following Jesus. Paul was so big a sinner that he called himself the chief of sinners. But very importantly, Paul explained that Jesus "came into the world to save sinners, of whom I am the foremost" (**1 Timothy 1:15**). So Paul understands the power of the grace of God through Jesus, and then he writes verse 6 in Romans 1, "[I]ncluding you who are called to belong to Jesus Christ." What a beautiful, beautiful verse. It is like God is speaking through Paul in this verse to us today (because He is) to join God's team. He is **calling** us to have a place of belonging— with the God who loves us. This sounds like a really good call. You see, now you can't say you were never called for anything good. This is the greatest call ever, and Jesus is calling your name!

These verses remind us of what Jesus did for us—He saw our need to be saved from sin, and He came. He died for us and rose again. Wow. Now He is calling us to belong to Him. The big question is how have you answered that call? That is the thing about being called: we have a choice whether to follow that call or not. When Jesus was on earth, sometimes people answered His call and followed (**Luke 5:1–11, Luke 5:27–32**), but sometimes they did not (**Mark 10:21–22, John 6:66–69**). What have you done in your life with this call to belong to Jesus? Some of you have accepted that call and have a new focus and purpose for life. If you have done that, then today's verses should be encouraging you to stand strong. This is the gospel. As many people say, we all need to remind ourselves of this gospel every day. Remembering what God has done for us and His second chances toward us will change how we live out this life for the better.

But some people don't accept this call. Some say they will think about it or accept Him later. This, of course, is a kind *No* but still just a *No*. Some people like where they are at—they like their sin. Sin is fun for a while, after all. Some people hold on to their unanswered questions too tightly and blame God for everything in their life that is bad, not realizing that the sin of the world is to blame for the bad, and God's grace is to credit for anything good. Others don't want to risk the change. Yes, Jesus will change your life if you let Him. For some reason, we all find change pretty scary, and we forget that this is *God* calling us, who truly loves the world (**John 3:16**). Jesus is pictured standing at the door to our life and knocking (**Revelation 3:20**). Will you let Him in? What will you truly do with this call?

I accepted this call when I was young. I was so young at the time that some would say I wasn't much of a sinner. BUT that isn't true since sin is sin, and I was just as much a sinner as anyone else. I started sinning at a young age, and I needed a Savior at my young age. Accepting Jesus let me have peace about my eternity and changed the direction of my life on earth toward Him. God wants your life to point in a new direction. He wants to help you through this life and carry you to Him after this life is over. Never forget that Jesus is calling you.

I hope you accepted His call. If so, be at peace today in your relationship with the God of the universe regardless of your present circumstances. He sees you. He loves us enough to have called us to Him even though we were far from him. This is amazing grace.

Day 82   Romans 8 (Part 1)

Romans chapter 8 is what I call an epic chapter of the Bible with many important thoughts, so we will spend the next few days going over them. I would encourage you this week to read the whole chapter through a few times, but today, I want to focus on one phrase from **Romans 8:1** and tell a story. The phrase is "no condemnation." That is big. This verse is telling us that if we are in Christ, God will not condemn us—that means He will NOT judge us guilty in life even though we deserve otherwise. Wow. We are free from condemnation. Think about that. What will we do with our new lease on life with God? We can do one of two things: we can live for God and make a difference in the world for Him, or we can use it as a free pass and waste His grace to us.

Last week, I watched a documentary on Netflix called *Q-Ball*. (It has since left Netflix but is available on other platforms.) I highly recommend it if you get a chance, and it is about basketball at a big prison in California. This was not a religious film, but the main character was changing his life through Jesus. There is a scene at a prison church service where this basketball star inmate shares a challenge to the crowd based on the man (Simon of Cyrene) helping Jesus carry the cross to His death at Calvary (**Luke 23:26**). He says that just like Jesus had help with His cross, so God is calling us to help Him and work for Him. Don't just sit there. Get up and do something for God. His grace has given us a second chance—don't accept it as cheap grace and do nothing for God. Jesus gave His life for you so change and give God your life. This was a strong scene with many inmates agreeing with the speaker that they needed to get up and serve God. God saved us by His grace, but do not waste your opportunity to now give your life for Him.

But in that scene in the film, there was one inmate who stood up in the service and called out, "Can Jesus carry my cross?" At first, this was confrontational to the message of the speaker, but what the second man was really saying was that he still needed Jesus to hold him and take care of him in life before he could serve God himself. So the speaker went to the man and said, "Yes, He can! Don't run from God but run to God." This second man cried, and they prayed for him in the service. So you can see that the movie was about a lot more than basketball. Anyway.

What we see here is Romans 8:1 lived out. No condemnation. What will you do with this second chance in life? It is like we have a long list of accusations by our name before God (and every one of us does), and God, the judge, rips up the list and says there is NO condemnation on you—you are free to live anew. That was the challenge. Don't ever take God's grace for granted and don't take it lightly. Take your new life and live it for God.

On the other hand, Romans 8:1 is simply an amazing comfort. There are times when we are very discouraged, and we can get down on ourselves. It is at these times that Jesus can lift the cross from off us, put His arm around us, and whisper, "You are not condemned." Wow. Romans 8:1 is both a challenge to us and is also an amazing comfort. God came to us—He sent His Son for us so that we would not be condemned. He has taken care of us.

I do not know where you are at with God today, but I know that if you are in Christ, if you give your life to Jesus, then you are not condemned for all of eternity. You are on God's team. That is freeing. That is humbling. That is amazing and challenging. I would encourage you to read one more story in the Bible on this topic. Read **John 8:2–11**. This also is a picture of God forgiving us so we can go forward and have new life. There is nothing in life more important than knowing God and accepting that you are not condemned in Him. Knowing that there is not a sentence hanging over you from God makes all the difference in the world. You need to humbly accept this. No condemnation! Let that phrase spread over you. It is not allowing us to keep sinning—it is allowing us to be free from the power of sin and be able to start again. There is not greater gift than a restart, and we have that in Christ. Rest in Him and go forward in Him.

Day 83   Romans 8 (Part 2)

Today we are going to take a deep dive into these first few verses of Romans 8, even though we already focused on verse 1 last time. Start by reading **Romans 8:1–8**. What stands out to you? What do you think it means to have your mind on things of the flesh or on things of the Spirit? What do we learn from these verses about God? What do we learn about man?

The end of the story is listed first in verse 1—that we are not condemned. The remaining verses explain how that happened for us. It clearly says that we are not set free from sin by the law or by the flesh. This is referring to works. Can you keep the law of God so perfectly that God sees your perfection and accepts you? No. Not one of us is perfect in comparison to God, but a lot of people (most) try to get to God by good works. Most people will find someone who is worse than them and say, "Well, I am better than that person, so I have a good chance of getting to heaven and God." This is so false! We think that God compares us to other people. Why would He do that? He is the standard; He is perfection; He is the Creator. So we think as long as I get a better grade than that guy, I am going to be okay (since that is how we got through school). But God grades simply on a pass/fail basis. You might be close, but it does not matter. You either pass or fail—and we all fail.

Now when we realize that we cannot work our way to God, we can do one of two things. A lot of people just try to erase God at this point. They might say, "Well, I don't even know if there is a God anyway." Why would they say this? Because they do not want to change; so if there is no God, then it doesn't matter what they do. Paul already addressed this in **Romans 1:18–23** (important verses). The other option is to leave the "mind of our flesh" (works) and set our mind on things of the Spirit **(Romans 8:5)**. How do we do this? We accept verse 3 as the truth. You see verse 3? That is the gospel, the good news. God sent Jesus—He looked like us but was perfect and conquered sin. So 8:4 tells us God was satisfied in Him, and He became the fulfillment of the law for us—which means He became our good works. In other words, what good works are you doing that will get you to heaven? There is only one answer—I accepted Jesus. So easy! And yet so many find it *so hard* to say they are not perfect, so they hang on to their works instead of God. Very sad. God is offering life and peace (verse 6) to us. Wow. Life, even though we failed God, and peace, even though we still struggle through this life. This is wonderful news. Why would we hang on to our own ideas and thoughts when God is offering us eternity and peace?

So these verses compare living with your mind focused on the flesh (this earth's stuff) or focused on the Spirit (the things of God and what really matters). You see, how we choose to go to God (works or faith in what He already did) will affect how we live now. If we stay just fleshly minded, we will live for this life—for money, pleasure, and good times for us (selfish). If we live according to the Spirit of God, then we will see that all that matters in this life is "loving God and loving the people He created" (Francis Chan). That is the true way of peace and how we can make it through this life. Imagine being able to give to people you know, maybe even your kids if you have any, the gift of a peaceful life and eternity with God. That happens by showing them who God is and living your life not according to this world's standards but keeping your mind on God. It is work. It sounds simple but is tedious and hard. But it is worth it. God is offering us the gift of no condemnation. That is such a freeing way to live.

Read **Romans 8:9–11**. Does this characterize you? Is Christ in you? Accept what He is offering you in verse 3. Maybe Christ is in you, but you have pushed Him down and cannot hear Him. Come on now—if you belong to Him, then that same Spirit of God who raised Jesus from the dead dwells in you. He will give you life right now—that is what verse 11 says. We need to do more living by the spirit. Do not let this world distract you from what really matters. Let God have His way with your heart rather than letting your heart get distracted by all the things in this world. What really matters? God and people. God is offering a way to help us see that in our lives. This is such wonderful news for us. Be encouraged in Him.

Day 84   Romans 8 (Part 3)

Today, we come to **Romans 8:12–18**. These are important verses about how we live and make it through this life. Sometimes you may not feel like you are going to make it—God wants us to know that we can make it through Him. Remember 8:1–11, which explains how God provided the way for us to escape the failure of our flesh because of Christ. Now we are not condemned, and we can go forward. Verses 12–18 give us some great thoughts about our new life in Christ.

1. Put to death your old life (v. 13). If Jesus came to save us from those wrong things we do in this body, then why would we go back to them? Be free from your sin. We were slaves to sin (verse 15). We need to step far away from sin, so we do not fall back into slavery. That picture is scary. It means sin can grab us and direct our lives while we feel incredibly helpless to that sin. So let's not go back to our sin. Stay far far away from the things that bring you down. You cannot play with sin. We often think we will be okay, nothing will happen, and go a little closer to our sin. We are good at making excuses to ourselves so we can go back in a tempting direction. No. This cannot happen. We have to put sin's power to death in our lives. This is possible, but we are going to need to run to God and stay very close to Him.

2. Run to God, your new Father (vv. 15–16). These verses say we do not need to fear our new Father, God, that He would be a slave driver to us. That was our old father, sin. Sin keeps us in slavery to it. Sin grabs us and does not want to let go until it ruins us. Think about that. Sin starts so fun—like a weekend party. Then we keep going back each weekend until we are addicted to the party, addicted to the high, addicted to the lifestyle. And it ruins us.

God is not like that! It says that God has adopted us as His children. That is huge. Adoption gives the idea He loves us so much that He went out of His way to bring us to Him. Adoption takes work and care—you don't have to adopt. It is harder to adopt a kid than having your own kid. And God loves us and wants us so much that He did the work through Jesus to adopt us into His family. We do not need to fear this Father because He loves us that much.

Now the Bible uses this imagery of Father a lot. Perhaps your earthly father was not a loving father. Perhaps your earthly father did not have much of a role in your life. Perhaps when you hear the word *father*, you have a lot of painful memories. I am sorry for that. But do not project those characteristics onto God. He is the perfect definition of Father. God wants to bring us that sense of belonging with Him that we cannot find elsewhere here on earth. We can truly trust Him for our lives. This can be a little scary for some of you—thinking of the future, are you ready to live for God? That is scary. But God our Father is going to be with you and carry you through the hard times that will come so we can be better. God loves us that much.

3. Suffering with God is SO MUCH better than suffering because of our sin (vv. 17–18). Wait a minute. Didn't I just write that life with God our Father is better than life without Him? Then why do the next verses talk about suffering? Because the Bible keeps it real. This earth is not paradise—that comes later, so hard times will be here. If we follow God, there will be opposition. Right now, some of you can think of some friends who will not be happy when you tell them you are not following their lifestyle anymore because you follow Jesus (you are ready to tell people that, right?). That will be hard. But verse 18 says so beautifully, "I consider that the sufferings of this present time are not worth comparing with the glory that is to be revealed to us." God has so much more for us in the future—to be with Him. The slight sufferings we will face now for making right, godly decisions here on earth are nothing in com-

parison to eternity with God. Always remember where we are headed—to be with God. That is what matters more than what anyone says or does to us here and now.

I encourage you to truly live out the new life in Jesus Christ. Put to death once and for all your old life of sin. We all need to do that each day. Run to God our Father each morning. Always look to Him when times get tough since He has us now and for eternity. Stay strong in Him.

Day 85   Romans 8 (Part 4)

Today and tomorrow, I want to finish some thoughts on Romans 8, and today are a couple very important verses, **Romans 8:28–29**. There is a promise in here that "all things work together for good…" That is a pretty huge statement. Can it be true? The answer is found in the context of that statement and what the word *good* means. What do you think it means?

Notice verse 28 starts with "for those who love God," so we see this verse only applies to those who are following Jesus and love God. Notice it does not say "for those who are living perfectly," because none of us would apply. But we do need to acknowledge God in our life, and if we have not been doing that, we should not expect this verse to work out for us.

Now, all things working out for good—what do you think that means? What does *good* mean? That is a loaded question. A small child would say that eating an entire carton of ice cream is good. But an hour later when that child has a big stomachache, was it really that good for him? We do need to acknowledge that compared to God, we are like that little child. Do we really know what is good for us? I would say that a million dollars would be really good for me. But what if I am irresponsible with the money, waste it, fight with my wife over the money (that happens now, right?), and have a miserable family life from now on because my wife and kids and I all fight over the money—is that good?

So the big question is what does God think is good? Well, we do not need to wonder. He tells us in verse 29. He says that those of us that have come to Him (and He knew about us from long ago—cool. He really loves us), God has destined us to be "conformed to the image of his Son." That phrase means to become like or look like His Son, Jesus. In other words, in God's eyes, good means we are becoming like Jesus. Think about that—becoming like Jesus—living like Jesus—doing what Jesus would do. It is best for us in our lives to be like Jesus—that is better than the million dollars. Be like Jesus!

The problem is that changes things. We might need to go through hard times in order to be more like Jesus. I mean, if I get that million and stop caring about other people because I got mine, then how is that making me more like Jesus? It isn't. Jesus showed love and forgiveness to people when they did not deserve it. You know what that means, right? The only way for us to show love and forgiveness to those who don't deserve it is for us to run into people who treat us wrong, and then show them love and forgiveness. Woah. Wait a minute. That is not good! And yet showing God's love to a world that does not deserve it *is* good. It is God who's good. And that is what God wants for us— to care and love rather than just get what we want for ourselves. Jesus went to the cross for us. You realize we are trying to be like the guy who wound up on the cross, not the ones putting Him there, right? We are not becoming like those who have power and abuse it. And we are not trying to *get* from others; we are trying to *give* to others.

Okay, but what about my life? What about when things go wrong for me—is all that God's fault? No, I can't say that. If I choose sin and it goes bad for me, I can't blame God. That is on me. But this is where I can turn to God and say, "I messed up. Please forgive me, and can you turn my mistakes into something good for you?" And this is where God says, "Yes!" Romans 8:28–29 shows us that God can take life and turn it for good—His good—which is to be more like Jesus. There is nothing better than that. Jesus suffered, but He was also happy when He ministered. He found joy in helping others. Imagine if we could live more like Jesus. If we did, this world would be a much better place, so let's start that. Let's live more like Jesus since that is what is best for everyone.

God saved us and destined us to be found in the image of Jesus—to look like Jesus. It might take time, and it might be a rough road to change us—well, it **will** be a rough road—but that is truly what is good for us. At the end of the day, I know that a million dollars is not as good for me as me changing as a person. Trust God and trust Romans 8:28–29; that He can take you and use your circumstances to help you be better—better like Jesus.

Day 86   Romans 8 (Part 5)

Today, we want to conclude with the end of Romans 8, so read **Romans 8:31–39**. What are your thoughts about these verses? Here are a few of mine.

1.   God is on our side (verses 31–34).

God is truly on our side. For real. You need proof? He "did not spare his own son" for us. God loved us so much that He came to us as Jesus (**John 1:14**) so that we could behold His glory, and so that he could save us from our sins. It says God gave us Jesus, so what more proof do we need that God is on our side? Not only that, He still cares for us and gives us (verse 32) what we need (see yesterday's devotional for background on that idea). Verse 33 says who can bring a charge against us? No one can, since God has already declared us innocent in Him because of Jesus. And verse 34 tells us Jesus died for us, rose again (read **1 Corinthians 15:1–10**), and is interceding for us—in other words, praying for us and caring for us and looking over us. Wow. So the only question is do you know Jesus because all of this is offered to us in Him. Hey, when you feel down, remember God is on your side and can still work in your life through all of the difficulties we have. I know this because of point 2 in this section.

2.   Nothing can separate us from the love of God (verses 35–36, 38–39).

There is nothing greater than God's love. He will love us and bring us to Him through all of life's problems. This life is hard, but God's love is greater. Now the list there implies that we might still go through tribulation (hard times) or distress or danger. Yes, these things are present. Later, it mentions rulers and higher powers—and none of this can separate us from God. In the middle of hard times, it is hard to believe this, but God wants us to know that whatever happens on this earth, He will keep His end of the bargain and bring us to be with Him for eternity. In eternity, the few years we have on earth will seem quite short, so we need to keep our eyes on Him and what is in store for us to be with God forever. Nothing can separate us from Him. Read **2 Corinthians 4:16–18**. I keep coming back to those verses because they are so important. Do not stay focused on the problems of this life but keep your eyes on eternity with God—to be forever with the one who truly loves you the most.

Also, what is keeping you from being closer to God right now? Do not let other people or your situation or even prison time keep you separated from the love of God. God is waiting here for you now. Keep repeating these verses with your situation in mind because it cannot separate you from God unless you let it. Stay close to Him each day because he is ready to pull you up. God is ready to love us in whatever state we are in because He knows our deepest sins (scary) and our terrible thoughts (also, scary), yet while we were sinning and were deep sinners, Jesus died for us (**Romans 5:8**). This is the unique and amazing message that the Bible brings us about God—that my failing works can't save me, only Him—and He loves me beyond what I can imagine.

3. We are more than conquerors (verse 37) because of His love.

This is the power of second chances. God loved us so much because He wants to *continually* give us another chance. He *still* loves us! Now think for a minute about who is writing this—the apostle Paul. He is saying that he too is more than a conqueror, but, remember, this is the same guy who a few verses earlier was saying that he constantly did what he did not want to do (**Romans 7:15**) and was so frustrated with his own actions, he said "wretched man that I am" (**Romans 7:24**). He is now saying he is more than a conqueror. I guess that means that God's love is enough for all of us too. We do not need to doubt God's love or think we have run out of chances. Nope. Because nothing can separate us from the love of God—not our sin or sin again or sin again. God loves a rescue story and loves showering us with His love so that we can become more than conquerors in this life and in eternity with Him.

Where are you at today? Feel like a conqueror? Probably not. I don't on most days either. That is why God had Paul write Romans 8—it is for us, all of us. We can all read this and realize who we are IN CHRIST. Jesus changes everything. Let Him change you too.

Day 87　　　　　　　　**John 3:30**

Today, I want to look at one verse. That's right—only one short verse. At the end of John chapter 3, John the Baptist (or Baptizer) is asked about the fact his followers are going to Jesus (**John 3:26**) instead of him. In response, John reminds them that his job was just to share that the Christ, the Messiah, was coming (**3:28**). Now that Jesus is known, John feels joy at that fact and says in **John 3:30**, "He must increase, but I must decrease." Think about that statement—it covers so much about our life. So why should Jesus increase in my life, and why should I decrease? I think of four reasons for this.

1. He should increase because He is worthy of the glory. God did not just say he loved me. He lived it. God became human flesh so I could understand His love for me (**John 1:14**), and so He could show me a better way to live. Jesus shows it all. Jesus is the end of me and beginning of new life because of Him. God has shown through Jesus what life is all about. The big questions—why am I here? What is my purpose for living? Since we have life through Jesus, He answers those questions—it is all for Him. When left to myself, I am lost (even though I think I am great and okay, down deep I know I am not). When I live for God, life has purpose beyond me that matters for eternity. That is because of the sacrifice of God for me. He is worthy of glory because of His love for me.

2. He should increase because he wants what is best for me. Did you see this phrase in point 1 above—"it is all for Him"? Here is the amazing thing. God loves us so much that when I give Him worship and live for Him, it actually benefits me, even right now here on this earth. We can find true peace and joy through Christ that we cannot find elsewhere, even though we try. People try to find good times for the weekend in a lot of ways, but Monday always

comes, and Monday's problems along with it. Jesus said that He came for us to have life and have it *abundantly* (**John 10:10**). That is quite a statement. God doesn't just want us to have eternal life (which is huge), but He also wants us to experience abundant life now. That happens through Jesus. He must increase. Let Him be the leader of your life (**Proverbs 1:7**).

3. I must decrease because, as Andy Stanley says, I have been involved in all of the bad decisions I have made. When I am the dominant factor in my life, it is often not good. I want what I want, and I often run over other people to get it. The more God is involved in my life, the wiser I am, and the better it is. I remember that the biggest person I cannot trust is me (**Romans 7:15, 21–23**). Wow. The more I study God's Word and follow the example of Jesus, the better life is for me. I need to get out of my own way. I must decrease.

4. I must decrease so that my pride decreases. God can come and fill my life with His wisdom and His joy, unless I am so full of myself that there is no room for God. This is related to the previous point but needs to be said. We often go through life pretty full of ourselves. For many people, our goal in life is to be The Man, so we make sure that everyone else knows who I am. Never apologize and never show weakness. This is pride. If other people are hurting, that is their problem—no, that attitude is pride too. I should care for others and sympathize with their problems even if their problems are not my problems. Pride keeps me from caring for others. Pride keeps me from being teachable and learning what God has for me. It is ironic that we think we have to fight for ourselves to go forward when actually that leaves us all fighting each other. The opposite of pride is the humility to realize that others have value, and I need to grow. Here are a few verses to help us see these thoughts:

Caring:	Mark 10:46–52	Matthew 9:35–36	James 2:1–6	Colossians 3:12
Humility:	Luke 22:24–27	Matthew 6:1–4	James 3:13–18	1 Peter 5:6–7

There are so many more verses than these, but I leave us with **James 4:10**. When we humble ourselves before God, He will take care of us. When we say, "I got this," God will let us get this—but that often ends poorly. Let God lead. Remember that He must increase, and we must decrease.

Day 88   Proverbs (Part 1)

For the next few days, I want to take a look at a few proverbs from the book of Proverbs. This book has so much wisdom that even now, a few thousand years after it was written, it still accurately describes life and people. Some of the proverbs talk about big themes, while others give random truth. Today, some themes:

1.   Watch your words.

If we could be careful with our tongue, so many problems would be solved. Read **Proverbs 10:19** and **11:13**. I feel like both of these verses could be rewritten as "just shut up." The first verse tells us sin is present when there are a lot of words. The more you talk, the better your chances of sinning. True. So if we would talk less, we could stay away from sin. Look at **Proverbs 17:28**—even a fool can seem wise if he would just shut up. Then verse 11:13 mentions slander, which is talking about other people. Nothing good comes from doing that. Gossip is talking about other people, even if it is true. That guy's life is not everybody's business. Give him a break and stop talking about him. The problem is we like gossip. **Proverbs 18:8** tells us those words people whisper to us (so no one else hears) are like tasty, delicious snacks. This is true, so we need to fight against all this gossip. It only leads to division and fighting.

Another aspect of our words is anger. **Proverbs 15:1** is so wise. When someone is getting angry, we can respond like he is—with angry words—and help make the argument even bigger. Or we can respond with a "soft answer," which will calm the situation down. Stay calm, answer calmly, and keep the peace.

2.   Be teachable.

This is a big idea in Proverbs and in life. Can you be taught? Are you open to change? Are you open to changing your life if God shows you new ways to live? This is so important. Read **Proverbs 9:7–9**. These verses contrast the scoffer and the wise man. The scoffer is one who makes fun of anyone who tries to teach him. He hates anyone who tells him he is wrong. This scoffer cannot be taught because he already knows it all. This scoffer is often so foolish that he thinks doing wrong is just a big joke—**Proverbs 10:23** says that! On the other hand, "Give instruction to a wise man, and he will be still wiser." There is wisdom in saying "I don't know everything." We have to be open to whatever God wants to teach us. We have to let Him guide us and not be offended at the idea that we need to change. We do. We always need to be changing and growing and becoming more like Jesus (see **Proverbs 12:1** and **13:1**).

3. Hang out with the right people.

Look at **Prov. 13:20**. If you hang out with wise people, you will be wiser. How about that! Choose good people to spend time with, and you will improve as a person. Yes. But if you hang out with fools, notice it does not say you become more foolish. It says you will suffer harm. You see, a fool does not care about the consequences for his foolishness. And if that fool does not care about himself, he certainly does not care about you. If you put yourself within the influence of a fool, you will find yourself drowning in the pool of his foolishness. If you are in a car of fools, you are all considered fools. And you will suffer harm. Please choose the right people to hang with. Just leave the wrong crowd (**Prov. 14:7**). Here are some more verses on this topic—**Proverbs 22:24—25, 27:17** (which shows how we can help each other be better), and **28:7**.

4. Be careful with alcohol.

The Bible does not say that drinking wine is a sin in itself, but there are many warnings about drunkenness. **Proverbs 20:1** tells us that "wine is a mocker." A mocker means it plays with us and fools us. We think that drinking our troubles away will take care of problems—no, the alcohol mocks us because the next day, all our problems are still there, and then some. The world does this with all kinds of things that promise us an escape from reality but actually enslave us in addiction. People look so cool in movies when they are drinking or at a drug party. If they can't handle it, well, they were weak, but I am strong. That is what we think, and we are fooling ourselves. **1 Corinthians 6:12** says that many things are not wrong (lawful) but are not helpful and can dominate me. Don't let alcohol or other items bring you under their power. Be wise. Stay close to God and be teachable. More tomorrow.

Today we cover an important topic that Proverbs gives lots of warning about: the wrong woman. You can start by reading the whole story of **Proverbs chapter 7**.

The first four verses are pleading with you to be wise and to keep this teaching written on your heart because you will need it. Why? Because of verse 5. We need this teaching to avoid "the forbidden woman…with her smooth words." Have you ever been with the wrong woman? You may not have known it at the time, but you found out soon enough…or maybe you did know she was wrong for you, but it was just going to be a little fun for a little while. Yeah, right. The Bible does not want us to chase the wrong woman, so we have this chapter as a warning. Look at the story again.

It starts with a "young man lacking sense." He is looking for some fun, so he specifically takes "the road to her house" in the evening under the cover of darkness (vv. 6–9). We already see some problems. This young guy (not much wisdom in his life) is playing with sin. He goes near sin by taking that street…he knows who is there. He walks toward the party just to see what might happen. He goes at dark—his friends and family don't know what he is doing. He is not accountable to anyone, which makes it too easy to hide what he is doing. This is us, right? We try to hide this stuff. We play with this stuff by going near it.

Starting in verse 10, we see the woman. She is not the kind of woman who would make a good wife, but she is a good time, and he is looking for that. I mean, she looks good dressed that way (v. 10). She is aggressive (v. 13)…this guy likes that. She was looking for him…her house is ready for action. She is easy (which is such a big warning sign, but anyway), and she is alone. Is there another man in the picture? Well, yes, but he is away, and she is talking so smoothly. Verses 22–23 say this guy is now like an ox going to slaughter. "He does not know that it will cost him his life." This is true. What will this night of pleasure cost the guy? Well, nine months from now, there might be a kid with a woman the guy doesn't really love—he was looking for fun and now has a lifetime of responsibility. Or he just has fun like this, but then a really good woman comes along and doesn't go for him because he has already slept with so many others. He missed out on a good woman because he fell for an easy woman. He thought he could get away with it because she said "stolen water is sweet" (**Proverbs 9:15–18**) but actually her house leads to hell on earth (7:27).

This chapter of Proverbs tells it like it is. All of this is true. Many men are blinded by outward beauty, and they do not pay attention to character and heart. Again, this woman is a good time but is not a good wife and is not a good life. If she is not faithful to her man now, what makes you think she will stay faithful to you? So what does matter most? Well, **Proverbs 31:30** says, "Charm is deceitful, and beauty is vain, but a woman who fears the Lord is to be praised." Does she love God? That is what matters most of all. Is she charming? Be careful. Is she beautiful? Doesn't matter, if her heart is not right with God.

Look, all men have issues in this area. If you have a good woman who loves God, then be a godly man for her. But if you are chasing the wrong woman (or women), then stop before it is too late. Never go for the woman who is easy; instead, chase the woman who is right with God (respect her, go to church with her, get to know who she is on the inside rather than physically). Take these warnings in Proverbs seriously.

What if you have already blown it in this area? Well, if there are kids, then show them that you are a man of God. They need to see you change so they don't repeat the cycle. Be a man of God that focuses on the spiritual instead of the physical. Be a one-woman man. God clearly established marriage as one man with one woman. Save the physical stuff for marriage. This is not what the world does, and they will think you are strange (read **1 Thessalonians 4:3–5 and 1 Peter 4:1–4** right now), but this is for our own good. Too many men chase a woman physically and later get burned. They were blinded by the physical, like the guy in Proverbs 7, and pushed aside the spiritual. Some guys have even stopped their faith because they are afraid their woman will leave them if they get too spiritual. That is such a sign that she is the wrong woman. Commit yourself to God first and be a man of God so you will attract a woman of God and not a woman of the world. There are many godly women out there. You be a godly man for their sake. I know this is a tough subject, but God's word keeps it real, so let's rest in God's grace and really work to honor God in the area of women.

Day 90   Proverbs (Part 3)

Today is our last day in this short series on Proverbs. There truly is so much wisdom in this book that I hope you read all of it on your own and find some truths that really speak to you. Now, some random thoughts that are still very important for our lives:

1. **Prov. 21:17.** Do not waste your money.

This verse literally tells us that if we love pleasure, we will be poor. Now we all love pleasure a bit. We all would love to have the nicer and finer things in life. We are constantly seeing those nice things on TV and around our neighborhood. We see that guy with the nice car, nice shoes, etc. So maybe we get some money—then we want that stuff too, but that will not truly help us. How many shoes do we need? Look, we need to save and take care of our money in order to take care of ourselves and others (our kids, especially). Ask yourself if you *really* need something before buying it. Do not overdo it. Look at **Prov. 25:16.** There is so much wisdom there—only use and spend for what you need. Save. Be wise and not wasteful.

2. **Prov. 24:16.** Get back up!

Have you heard people tell you that if you do what is right, then everything will be great for you? What a joke, right? Can you think of time that you did what was right and still got in trouble? The Bible does not promise everything will work out smoothly for us every time here on earth. Jesus faced a lot of injustice. But it did not stop Him. This verse tells us that the wicked man falls and quits. The righteous man falls and gets back up. It is true. We have to be men that do not let life stop us. We have to get back up and do right when we fall. Isn't this the power of God's grace anyway? God gives us His grace so that we <u>do</u> have the power to get up when we fall. Do not stay down, and do not let life get you discouraged. The righteous man is not perfect. But the righteous man will get back up and keep going on the right path.

3. **Prov. 25:17.** Do not take advantage of others' generosity.

This is kind of a funny proverb but true. Sometimes we need the help of others, and we should take it. If God sends help along, accept it. Sometimes we get stubborn and refuse help when we need it. BUT then sometimes we take too much from others—guess what? They will get mad at us if we do that. This verse tells us not to go too often to our neighbor's house, lest he hate us. I like the phrase "lest he have his fill of you." That means he can only take so much of you before he gets tired of you. How do we combat this? Be humble. Be gentle. Don't be loud and rude, or else you will get on others' nerves.

4. **Prov. 25:21–22.** Be kind to your enemies.

Here is a principle that Jesus also emphasized. The phrase in verse 22 could be translated, "Be kind to your enemies because it will blow their minds." Look, this gets at the heart of who followers of Jesus truly are (read **Matthew 5:43–48**). Anyone can be kind to nice people. It takes a special person to be kind to a jerk. But that is what God has called us to—because we are all jerks to God—we are sinners!—and yet God still loves us and cares for us. This is where God wants us to show His kindness to others. God has forgiven us, so we need to be ready to forgive others (Read **Matthew 18:21–35**).

5. **Prov. 25:28.** Control yourself.

Self-control is so important. Here, it says a man without self-control is like one of those old ancient cities that defended itself with a big wall, but the wall is broke. The city might be strong and wealthy, but without the wall, that city is open to destruction. In the same way, we have skills and abilities, but our lack of self-control in some area can destroy us. We can be doing so well in some ways, but there is this thing we always give in to. Maybe it is a desire that all our money goes to or maybe a drug. Maybe it is anger or women. Whatever it is, our whole life can come crashing down when we do not control that impulse. God knows this. He says we have to control ourselves and war against the passions and desires that are in the world and in us but will bring us down (**1 Peter 2:11**). Even good things become bad for us in excess. Look at the verse right before this: **Prov. 25:27**. Don't eat too much of a good thing. Don't seek your own glory. Control yourself and let God fill your heart.

Keep reading Proverbs, and may God guide and bless!

Holiday Devotionals

Day 91   Thanksgiving

Thanksgiving. It is one of the biggest holidays in our country, but I do not write very boldly today, though, because what can I say? Some of you might think I am about to write that you should be thankful for what you do have, blah, blah, blah. But let's be honest, I don't think too many people are thankful for hard times and being in jail. I know that I have a hard time being thankful when things aren't going perfectly for me—why should I be thankful for hard times? So this is a hard topic when life is going wrong. All I can do is look to what God says about thankfulness in difficulty and trust that it is true.

The classic verse on thankfulness is **1 Thessalonians 5:18**, which says, "Give thanks in all circumstances; for this is the will of God in Christ Jesus for you." Hmmm. There is something about that phrase "all circumstances" that is troubling because that means I need to give thanks when things are bad. I need to give thanks when things don't go my way. But why would I do that? I am thankful when things are easy for me and when things are going smoothly. Why does God want me to be thankful at *all* times?

Maybe the answer is found in **James 1:2–4**. It says here I should consider it "joy" when I "meet trials of various kinds." I should be happy that life sucks? Well, yes. Why? It says that this is a testing of my faith, which "produces steadfastness" and eventually makes me "perfect and complete." The testing of my faith makes my faith stronger and makes me a better person in God, so I should be thankful for the difficult times. That's what it says anyway. I guess I think of a baby starting to walk. That baby falls down a lot (it is okay, the diaper provides enough padding for a soft landing) and has to learn to get back up. Imagine if a baby tried to walk once, fell down, sat there, and said, "That's it, never doing that again." If that happened, that baby would now be a man sitting in the same spot, maybe with the same diaper on! For the baby, each failure at walking is a step in the process. Is that what God is saying about our faith here?

Romans 5:3–5 says the same idea. We should "rejoice in our sufferings" because they are producing endurance, character, and hope. It says hope "does not put us to shame" because God pours out His love into our hearts. I guess this says I should rejoice and be thankful in hard times because that is when I can look forward to God showing me His love more. I like the idea of getting God's love, but that still doesn't really make me thankful for hard times.

In **2 Corinthians 12:7–10**, the apostle Paul shares his personal testimony of hardship. He had something (thorn in the flesh) that really bothered him and kept him down. He asked God three times to remove it…wait. He "pleaded" for its removal. I think this means there were three times he spent like a day pouring out his soul before God to remove this thorn, whatever it was. And each time, God said no. But with the no, God said that His grace is enough. He said that Paul's weakness would let God show His strength. So, in the end, Paul praises God for his weakness, insults, and hardships. Paul says that when he is weak, that is when God comes along the most in showing His strength.

Somehow, Paul was thankful even though God said no to him. That is deep thankfulness. Paul mentions this is one other verse, **Philippians 4:11–12**, where he says he has learned to be content in every situation, even when facing hunger and need. How? I think his eyes were always on Jesus, no matter what. His focus was never on his struggles but always on the long-term eternity with God.

So there we go; I cannot claim to be thankful like Paul. I cannot tell you to be thankful like Paul. All I know is that somehow, he found a way. I do not know the details of your situation, but I know that God sees you, and according to these verses, He can use what you are going through to grow you as a person in Him. He wants you to be "complete" in Him and is ready to shape you to be a little more like Jesus, if you let Him. It is not easy, but in the long run, maybe God is truly changing you through these hard times. If God has not given up on you and is shaping you to be better for Him, then that is something to be thankful for. I pray you can find your peace and joy in knowing God at this Thanksgiving time, even in the midst of pain. May we rejoice in His strength; not ours. God bless.

Day 92　　　　　Christmas (Part 1)

Christmas is coming, and I am sure that this will be a hard week for many of you. I do not want to add sadness to the fact you are here for Christmas, but I hope that somehow you can find your encouragement in Christ in spite of your location. The whole reason there is a Christmas at all is because of Jesus Christ (not Santa), and we want to properly understand what God was doing for us at this time. Today, I want to focus on two verses, **John 1:14** and **Galatians 4:4–5**. These verses tell us what we need to know about why Christmas happened and why it is meaningful spiritually.

I read this little story that helps us understand what Christmas is really all about. There once was a farmer who every morning would go out to his barn and get birdseed. He would scatter the birdseed on his grassy yard, and many birds would come eat. The birds got used to being fed by the farmer and waiting for him at dawn each day. Well, one day the farmer was extra tired; he went into his barn to grab the birdseed but picked up a bucket of rat poison by accident. He threw it onto his yard, and the birds flocked to eat. As the farmer went back into the barn, he realized his deadly error, so he ran outside and chased away the birds. Except they did not leave. The birds kept eating because they knew the routine and could not understand that something was wrong. The frustrated farmer kept trying to stop the birds, but it was no use. They didn't get it. As the birds ate the poison, the farmer looked up and yelled, "If only I could become a bird so they could understand me, and I could warn them!"

This story is a picture of what happened at Christmas. God is so far above us that it is impossible for us to truly comprehend Him. But He loves us so much that He came down here. He became us so we could understand His message. John 1:14 says, "The Word became flesh and dwelt among us, and we have seen his glory, glory as of the only Son from the Father…" We could not see and understand God's glory and love for us until that love came to earth as a man, as us. What does grace really mean? It is found in Jesus—how

He loved people, cared for people, and went to the cross for us sinners. What is truth? God is truth. God is there and wants us—this is why Jesus came. This is what Jesus showed us, since John 1:14 also says that "his glory...from the Father" was "full of grace and truth." Christmas is our understanding who God is and how much He cares for us. It is Him coming down so we can be saved from the poison of sin, just like that farmer wanted to warn the birds about the poison in their lives.

This is God's plan and was God's plan from the beginning. His plan when we sinned was not to make us pay for it; we could never pay enough to a holy God for our sin. So God decided He would pay for our sin. He would need to become one of us to do so. Galatians 4:4–5 says that when the time was right, "God sent forth his Son, born of woman, born under the law." Jesus was God become man. And why did God do this? That last phrase of Galatians 4:5 tells us: "So that we might receive adoption as sons." That is pretty big talk. Adoption. We were lost and homeless, orphans for eternity, living for nothing but ourselves—and God adopted us. He wanted us so much that He paid the price to let us come to Him. He did not change His character of holiness; He just made sure that the payment for sin was made. By Jesus. For us. Now we are sons of a true Father. A Father who always is there for us. A Father who was willing to sacrifice Himself for us.

That right there is Christmas. Christmas is the fulfillment of God's plan to make it easy for us to be saved. Adam made it easy for us to sin; Jesus made it easy for us to go back to God. **Romans 5:17** says: "For if, because of one man's trespass, death reigned through that one man, much more will those who receive the abundance of grace and the free gift of righteousness reign in life through the one man Jesus Christ." There it is—a free gift—from God—embodied in that baby Jesus who would grow to be our Savior. Christmas is about God's love. Christmas is about gifts because of God's gift. Christmas is about heaven. Christmas is about God providing hope for us in spite of the poison of our sin. Death does not need to be the end of our future. We can rest in that "abundance of grace," and we can be in amazement that God would offer us "the free gift of righteousness." Christmas season can be hard when we are not with loved ones or don't have loved ones. Rest in the fact that you are the loved one of God.

Day 93   Christmas (Part 2)

Today, a few more thoughts on Christmas. Hopefully by focusing on the Savior, we can find some joy in this season. Let's read the most famous passage on the Christmas story, which is **Luke 2:1–20**. I want to point out three thoughts today:

1. Jesus came for everybody. We read the story and think it is pretty cute to have the shepherds involved. It seems fitting that shepherds would be visiting the baby Jesus at the manger. Shepherds already work with animals so, of course, they would visit. But we need to really think about why shepherds and who these men were.

In society back then, people were pretty concerned with who you were because people wanted to try to move up the social ladder (kind of like today!). Think about the Pharisees who looked down on so many other people (and drew the most scoldings from Jesus because of this fact) and did not want to associate with people below them. Can you imagine if Jesus came to earth in a Pharisee house? The religious leaders would have refused entry to most other people who wanted to see the baby Savior. So it is significant that God wanted these shepherds to hear about the Savior first. The shepherds were looked down on by society, but not by God. God sent His angels to tell the shepherds because God cared for the poor and the lowly people. Jesus was born in a stable, a barn! Anyone was welcome to visit, but I am sure rich people and "religious" people of that day would not have wanted to go to a barn. The shepherds, on the other hand, were excited to go and see what God was doing. God cares about everybody. He wanted the lowest of society, the shepherds, to know for sure that they were cared about. So they are the ones chosen to hear about Jesus first. This is actually wonderful news for all of us. We can all know that God cares for us, no matter who we are.

2. Do not fear. This statement is said so many times in the Bible, and here again it is said, this time by the angels to the shepherds. Why would the shepherds be afraid? Well, they just saw these angels in the sky, right? That is highly unusual. But also, there was a message given that was supposed to be great joy. A Savior had arrived. THE Savior. That means a lot. That means lives will change. That also means my life will change. Hmmm. That can be scary. It is interesting how much we don't like change. Many people would rather accept a fairly miserable life than change—why? Because what if my life gets worse? At least I know this life now. But that sets the bar of success so low. God wants us to succeed and thrive in life—He really does. God knew that change for the better starts with taking care of our sin problem once and for all. We fail at keeping the law and really need some way to get out of the rut of sin. God provides it. He provides us with grace and forgiveness through a Savior, Jesus.

Some people owe money. Then their plans fail, and they can't pay it back. That debt just keeps growing. Eventually, the only way out is just to wipe it clean and start over. That doesn't happen too much in the real world. BUT it does happen with God. God is willing to wipe our slate clean and let us start over. This is huge. It can be scary because that old life is all we know. But this is where God says don't be afraid. Accept Jesus. Then go forward in a new life with Jesus. This is the true message of Christmas. And it is wonderful. Do not fear change with God. It is *with God*! No fear.

3. It is a message to tell. At the end of this passage, the shepherds went and told others that the Savior was here. They did not tell the message yelling at people. No, they simply, humbly shared the good news of a Savior, of God's love come to earth. The Christmas message is not Santa. The Christmas message is not lights or holiday feelings. The Christmas message is that our lives can be saved and

changed because God provided a way of forgiveness. He did not provide it merely in words. No, He provided His very Son as God in the flesh to be a sacrifice for us. This Savior is a gift to us. A gift! (**Ephesians 2:8–9, Romans 6:23.**) Jesus is the first and best gift of Christmas. The best way to show that you care for others is to share about that gift.

So, yeah, I know that Christmas in here is hard. Yet I hope you can still find a way to celebrate with the One who originated Christmas in the first place: God, who sent Jesus. May we hold tight to God's gift to us at this time of year. Merry Christmas because of Him.

Day 94   New Year. New You (Part 1)

January 1. I am not big on new year resolutions, but I do use this time to take a real look at where I am in life. I also like thinking about a few life goals to keep in mind for the next year and beyond. So this week we will think about the new year. Today we will look at the spiritual side, and next time we will look at some practical applications of that.

According to **2 Corinthians 5:17**, if you are in Christ, you are a new creation. New! "The old has passed away; behold, the new has come." Every one of us, listen, every one of us needs to rest in this newness in Christ and move forward in this newness. We need to show it and live it. How? Read **2 Corinthians 5:14–21**. Here are a few thoughts:

1.   Accept His righteousness (verse 21). Are you right with God right now? Have you accepted what Jesus did for you so that when you stand before God you can point to Jesus as your representative rather than yourself? That is where it all begins. This is the time to get right with God.

2.   Be under Christ's control and not under your "old self's" control. What do I mean? Look at verse 14. It says that the love of Christ now controls us. Why do we do what we do? Because of Jesus. It is Him. We do not live for ourselves (verse 15) but for Him. Why? Living for ourselves doesn't work. Who are we? Sinners. Living for self will always lead to a bad end. Look at **Romans 6:6–16**. Our old self was a slave to sin. Jesus died for that sin to wipe the slate clean so we can start over with God. This Romans passage keeps saying that sin leads to death. It does. Sin leads to both eternal death and misery here on earth. Do not believe the lies sin tells you. Put yourself under God's control.

3.   Back to 2 Cor. 5:14–15. What is it describing when we read "the love of Christ controls us"? That is describing a

relationship. The Christian life is not a set of rules but is a relationship with God through Jesus and because of Jesus. It starts with His love for us, and that relationship grows because of our love for Him. Why? Because He has freed us from a life of sin. His grace and mercy are new every day. That is huge. We don't memorize a list of things not to do to stop sinning—no, we just need to remember who loves us and live for Him. In that way, we will avoid sin—because of this love relationship with God.

So as you look forward into the new year, here are a few things to keep in mind:

- Look forward! Stop looking back unless you need to make some things right. Our old self was crucified with Jesus, so we do not need to look back. Go forward.
- Love God. As we remember His love for us, we will grow in our love for Him. It is a *relationship*.

God really wants to renew your life and mine. It does not matter where we are in life, we can go forward with Him. Do you need to start over with God? He is ready to let you do that (which is amazing). Think about it, God really wants us to be free from our past and start over. He wants us to be free to start over from last year to this year and even from yesterday to today.

There is a song by Flame feat. NF called "Start Over" I close by sharing some of the lyrics:

> Everybody's got a blank page; A story they're writing today; A wall that they're climbing; You can carry the past on your shoulders; Or you can start over; Regrets, no matter what you've gone through; Jesus, He gave it all to save you; He carried the cross on His shoulders; So you can start over
>
> See, His love is deeper than the ocean floor; Run to His arms like an open door; God the

Father sent the Son; So men can come and be free and ain't gotta run no more (that's what He said); Come to me, all who are weary; with heavy burdens, I'll give you rest; Separated you from your sin, as far as the east is from the west (He said) Thrown in the sea of forgetfulness; What sin? What offense? And when them waves come crashing in, I'll calm the winds in your defense (that's what He said); So, whatever it is that you've done; He put that punishment on His Son; You'll never come under His condemnation. Conquer sin and Satan, and his accusations; So, dry your eyes, lift up your head; Hallelujah! God is not dead! Plus, He gave us His peace, and He took our guilt on the cross instead; Took our place and now we embrace; A clean slate with the eyes of faith; We know unfailing love, unfailing love, it's not too late, start over.

Day 95   New Year. New You (Part 2)

Yesterday, we looked at how God's amazing grace allows us to start over. Really. We can draw a line (God's grace), give the past over to God, and go forward. Actually, when we meet God through Jesus, this is exactly what God wants to do—to renew us and make us new. Read **Ephesians 4:22–24**. Those are some powerful verses about your "new self." I want to look into that a bit more, but today I want to stir up your thinking about some goals you might make for yourself in the new year. These goals should be spiritual AND practical. Don't miss out on the fact that we need to live in the real world and need to be renewed in how we handle life. Here are six ideas for you facing the new year:

1a. Be teachable. Read **Proverbs 9:7–9**. A wise man listens and gets wiser. A foolish man does not want to learn, so verse 8 says that that fool (a scoffer) will hate anyone who tries to teach him. Don't be a fool. Learn from life and learn from God. Be teachable.

1b. Have time with God each day. So this point is a part of number 1 because the time we need to be most teachable is when we are reading God's word or listening to a sermon or even learning from songs. Whatever you do, spend a few minutes with God each day—be thinking about these verses we look at on these pages and be praying to God. If you don't know what to pray for, just pray for yourself and people around you. Also, you can tell God you don't understand life and ask for His guidance (**James 1:5**). This does not need to be a superlong time, but every day you skip time with God, it becomes easier to push God away the next day/week/month/lifetime. Let Him teach you. Make time for God.

2. Establish routines and order in your life. This is a practical goal. When will you spend time with God? Keep that

appointment with Him. When you get out of here, have routines in your life. Order is proven to be a way successful people stay successful.

3. Grow in the fruits of the Spirit. **Galatians 5:22–23** tell us nine fruits. When we say "grow" in God, we mean grow in these things—grow in love, faith, joy, and patience. Ask God to strengthen you in these areas and look for ways to act more gentle and kind. Spend time deepening your faith in God.

4. Goals. Make them. Have them. Review them. Follow them. Each day, take at least five to ten minutes to move toward your overall goals. These goals should be spiritual, emotional (intellectual), and physical. We get the physical goals easily (and we should be in good physical condition), but we need spiritual goals to get closer to God and other goals to move toward a job and caring for loved ones around us. Get rid of things and people that interrupt the flow of your life and stay stable and steady in your future goals.

5. Be ready to do hard things. Jordan Peterson wrote, "Vice is easy. Failure is easy too. It's easier not to shoulder a burden. It's easier not to think, and not to do, and not to care." Wow. This is true. It does not take effort to fail, and it does not take effort to not help. It is easy to be lazy. It is hard to be successful. It is hard to grow in character. It is hard to grow deeper in your walk with God. Example: It is also hard to shoot like Steph Curry on a basketball court—that is why he spends hours on the court practicing (by the way, he hit 105 corner three in a row in a workout once—there is video proof). In the same way, you do not become better at being a person without effort. Put work into becoming a better person. I can be lazy in my relationships with my family, for example. I need to keep at being patient and giving time to my kids. I need to reach out and give time to others and help others. Sometimes I would rather be lazy, but nothing good comes of that. Do hard things.[3]

6. Love others. Love is a fruit of the Spirit. Jesus also emphasized love over and over again. He said this would be the way that people know we are His followers (**John 13:34–35**). Who can you show love to? Who needs to know that someone cares for them? What is a way that you showed someone that you give a care today? It is easy not to care. It is easy to say "they are not my business." Do not take that easy road. Show someone that they mean something to God by caring for them yourself. God loves and cares for every person, even if we don't. Wow. How can you show others you have the love of God in you each day?

Think about all this. Make some goals. May God empower you. He can.

---

3   Peterson, Jordan B., *12 Rules for Life: An Antidote to Chaos* (Toronto: Random House Canada, 2018), 78.

Day 96　　　　New Year. New You (Part 3)

I trust God is guiding, and you are thinking about what areas God wants to change you. That is exciting to think about as we head into a new year. God wants every one of us to be better in Him. God has been having me really think about these verses we looked at previously, so now we will look in more detail at **Ephesians 4:17–24**. Read those verses and take a moment to think and retell in your own words what you think God is saying here.

1. "Futility of their minds" (v. 17). This is the first phrase that stands out to me. "Futility" means "what is the point? There is none. This is a waste of time." This verse tells us that without God, there is no real purpose to life. It is saying that all the world offers us is empty promises. Is that true? Think about what the world offers us—parties, getting wasted, shallow relationships—what is the point? Is life about a good time this weekend? Then what? Is life about finding ways to forget the weekend and my past mistakes? Look, everything the world offers us to follow is futile. There is no point. Meaningful living and meaningful relationships can happen through Jesus. When we are "renewed" and living after the "likeness of God" (v. 24), life matters more and comes together. When we know where we are headed in life tomorrow (eternity with God because of Jesus), then we can get through life today. We need to realize that each day comes down to what we are living for, and when we live for Jesus (as a new person in Him), everything else can come together. Without God, we will run into trouble. I know this sounds a little "preachy," but I am burdened that too many people are just wandering through life with no purpose. God created us and getting back to our Creator gives life purpose.

2. "Due to their hardness of heart" (v.18). This passage is describing the old man—who people are before they meet God. It says that they are "darkened in their understanding." This means they do not understand God, they do not understand life, they do not understand the best way of living, which is in God. But why don't they understand? "Hardness of heart." They do not *want* to understand. People that are living apart from God often ignore God on purpose. Think about that guy who is making the wrong choice again—he knows what he is doing and knows how this is going to turn out, but he refuses to think that through because he just wants to live for the moment. People shut God out of their lives on purpose, and sadly fall into deeper and deeper holes. Do not let your heart get hard against God. Maybe even reading this book has become old to you, and you do not want to really think about it. God is saying in this very passage that we need to be renewed in Him all the time. He does not want us to be ignorant on purpose. God knows that being renewed in Him is the best answer for my life. That is why He sent Jesus.

3. "Greedy to practice every kind of impurity" (v. 19). This is what the world offers us. Impurity of every kind. I do not need to explain this point. Impurity is around us all the time in many different ways. It is ultimately futile to live for impurity. Giving in to our sinful nature drags us away from a meaningful life. Following what God has for us and resting in Him is truly meaningful.

4. "Renewed in the spirit of your mind" (v. 23). Here is the key. When we accept Jesus and decide to live for God, we have a new mind—a new way of thinking. We start to see what really matters in life. And, by the way, what matters in life is loving God and loving the people He has created. We can only truly love other people when we accept God's love for us. When we understand God's love, a love that went to the cross for us sinners (**Romans 5:6–9**), then we can accept others where they are at and help them make better

decisions in God. When we are renewed in our thinking, we see what really matters in life. Look at it this way; if I have a four-year-old son and give him a ball, then we can play together all afternoon. The four-year-old thinks it is all about the ball—he might look for another ball and play with someone else and find it isn't as fun. Why? Because it was never about the ball. The father realizes it is about the relationship and giving his kid some precious time and a memory. Sometimes we go around life chasing things and good times like the four-year-old but never get it. Because it is not about the ball. It is about the relationship. The relationship with God. Your old self is focused on the wrong things. We can get a new self in Christ, which leads us to true meaning in life. May this year be the year we are renewed in our relationship with God.

We have been thinking about how a new year can be motivation for a new you and new me. We have seen that a "new self" starts with God getting rid of the old me and then me letting God change me. The world offers us futility, while God offers real meaning and real change. We will keep looking at our passage today as we define that change and new self. Read **Ephesians 4:17–32.**

The verses 25–32 help define what we are changing. These are specific examples of ways we change when we are living that new life in Christ. What stands out to you in the list? Which one or two are important for you to follow? Okay, I am not going to explain the list but try to see if we can summarize it. It tells us here the following commands:

- Tell the truth.
- Don't keep your anger. Deal with it and don't drag yesterday into today.
- Live honestly.
- Let your words be encouraging and uplifting to other people.
- Rather than staying angry and bitter for weeks, months, or years, forgive and treat others kindly.

Look at that list. What is it really saying? All of those things involve our relationships with other people. This is telling us to care about others. We are naturally pretty selfish, but God wants us to change. If I don't tell the truth, I am actually manipulating information so that I stay ahead of the other person. I lie so that I can still look good before others when I don't deserve to. My anger is all about me—it is all about what you did to me, and we are not even until I get you back. This attitude gives an opportunity to the devil (v. 27) to poison my life. I can be consumed with hate and revenge, and then what? Nothing good is happening there. Why am I angry?

Because to me, my name is more important than yours, and you disrespected me. We need to make that even, so I am looking to pull you down rather than giving you over to God.

Keep going. Live honestly—again, when I am dishonest, it benefits me, but it hurts you. I don't care about you, so I am willing to cheat to get ahead of others. Hey, I need to look out for myself any way possible, right? No, I need to give myself over to God. My words—too often, my words are a way to lift myself above you. I want to tear you down, so I go up. God tells us to encourage each other instead. Bitterness sets in when I do not give past hurts over to God. That is huge. Forgiveness is not just for you; it is also for me. I need to forgive so I don't become consumed by you. Imagine that—I can get so angry with someone that they are all I think about. Wow, now who is controlling whom? I am letting that other person dominate my thinking rather than just giving them over to God so I can move forward. Forgive.

Ephesians 4:32 is so important. It summarizes my renewal in Christ. I am no longer so concerned with my status. Instead, I am tender to you. I care for you. I can care for people I don't even know that well because I know that God cares about those people. A tender heart is a gentle heart. And yes, men can have gentle hearts. Men can be leaders in caring. Absolutely. **Don't be so concerned with being THE man that you forget what it means to truly be A man.** Women and kids are looking to us men to be caring, but way too often, we get caught up in the bitterness of holding grudges and the race of beating others in life. Stop. These verses are calling us to care about others like God cares about us.

That is the root of all of this—you know that, right? God could have just wiped us out for being sinners. God should have just wiped us out for being sinners. Instead, God reached out to us even while we were being sinners. Jesus was willing to be abused by those who rejected Him in order to reach the few that would accept Him. They were worth it. We were worth it to Him. So when verse 32 says that God forgave us in Christ, He is showing us our path to a new life and new self. Care about people like God cared about you. That is our challenge this new year.

I hope you are taking time to think and pray about how God wants you to be renewed. Change is scary, but God is so ready to help us because He loves us and knows what is best for us. May He be guiding you.

Day 98   **New Year. New You (Part 5)**

When you were young, was there anyone you wanted to be like? When we are kids, I think we love those superhero movies and want to be one of them—we imagine ourselves with superpowers. As we grow older, we usually look up to those who are slightly above us; like when I was in eighth and ninth grade, I looked up to the eleventh and twelfth graders in high school. They were cool, right? As we go along in life, we do actually have a big decision in life to make—who do we want to be like? Who will be our role model? A few facts about role models need to be said:

1. If we are honest, we all have role models, even if we just take one or two qualities from them.
2. We can get role models from people we know or celebrities in the media or from stories we hear from the street.
3. If we are searching for a role model to justify our bad behavior, we will find him.
4. The reality is that too few men have a positive male role model in their lives. Many men in our lives have failed us.

So what do we do with this? Heading into the new year, how can I be a new man when I don't have someone to follow? How can I see what a new life looks like when no one in my life is living a new life? The answer is found in **Ephesians 5:1–2**. God became man, Jesus, so He could save us from our sin, but also so He could leave us an example of a real man. He lived in our shoes so we could see it be done. Who should be our role model? Answer: Jesus and anyone else who is trying to be more like Jesus in his life.

Verse 1 says we should be imitators. We should be trying to copy someone. Here it says to be an imitator of God as shown in the life of Jesus. Verse 2 gets specific about the fact Jesus showed us the way of sacrifice and love. Can we think about that a minute? What does that mean? That means living a life of inconvenience. It means I need to out others first in my life. I might say, "Well, they don't care about me." Okay, have you given them a reason to? Why can't you start caring for them first? When we as men start to care for others, lives can be changed, and people will show that same love and respect back at us. But we need to do it first. We can't say "I will treat them better when they start treating me better" because if we all say that, there will be no change. This is the definition of a leader—**being someone who is willing to make the change first**. That means I need to follow these verses and lead in love first. That is what God did toward us—He did not wait for us to turn to Him before showing His love to us. "We love because He first loved us" (**1 John 4:19**). Make Jesus your role model—He loved people before they realized who He was. He cared for people who could never pay Him back. He did not follow the endless cycle of revenge. Revenge only leads to everybody being hurt—you realize that, right? Jesus saw that and told us to be leaders in stopping the pattern of revenge (**Matthew 5:38–42**).

But what do we do? We follow the wrong role models. The next verses talk about this. Read **Ephesians 5:3–8**. This is our world—especially sexually immoral and impure. Those are the role models we are given in society—that the cool one has lots of women and money by whatever means possible. This lifestyle is praised in music and movies. We are told by the world a real man follows his heart, but these verses show us where that will lead. Look at verses 6–7. Don't be deceived, it says! Don't fool yourself into looking at the godless world and saying that is an acceptable lifestyle. It says "do not become partners with them." Do not have a role model that is a person who does not love Jesus. You are deceiving and tricking yourself if you believe success is women and money.

That brings us back to Jesus. True success is letting people know you care. True success is giving people your time and praying for them. In **John 4**, Jesus sat with this lady who was a sinner sleeping around. He cared for her soul. He wanted her to see that chasing men was not working for her. A life following Jesus was the answer. Are you looking for true peace this year? Are you looking for true success this year? Are you looking to be a new man this year? The only way to all of that is living a life like Jesus. Pour your heart into getting to know Him better and then live it out. Ephesians 5:1–2 is real, for real.

Today, read **Ephesians 5:15–21**. Looking ahead in your life, follow the words of verse 15 so you can live "not as unwise but as wise." Have you ever done something and said to yourself "That was dumb"? I do that all the time. These verses challenge us to slow down and "look carefully" at how we live. These verses give us a plan forward and a way to live wise from this point on. Take a look at what they say to us:

1. "Look carefully." Really. Take time to look at yourself. Be honest with yourself. Face your weak areas and work on them. As a basketball coach, I can't say, "Our team is weak at this, so we will ignore that area of the game." No, I need to look at our team's weaknesses and address them to change them. So too we need to look carefully at ourselves to address areas we need to change. Look carefully.

2. Make the best use of time. That is a good statement too, but wait a minute, how can we make best use of our time now, here? That is a good question. Do you have a plan for the next ten years of your life? Do you have a plan for the next one year of your life? Are you thinking about that? We should be moving toward those goals each day. Where do you want to be in life? Wait, more importantly, what kind of person do you want to be in life? Are you becoming more like Jesus today? Yes, even today can be used to increase our knowledge of God and grow in what matters (**Colossians 1:9–11**). I challenge you to take some time each day while you are here to carefully consider God and get to know Him better. That is not a waste of time but is making the best use of our time.

3. Don't be foolish, but know His will (v. 17). There is a line between having a good time the right way and foolishness. Don't cross it. Kids fool around a lot, especially middle

schoolers, but too much of that does not help us mature and grow up to be men. Search God's word for how He wants us to live—that is good use of our time because the days are evil (v. 16). Be ready to follow God in evil days.

4. Be controlled by God (v. 18). You can be controlled by God or not. The example here is alcohol. The Bible does not forbid drinking, but it does tell us not to be drunk. Why? Because we are out of control. We cannot make good decisions when we are drunk—we become slaves to drink or to whatever we are taking that is clouding our minds. You might need to say no to drinking totally because you are giving over control of your life to the bottle of whatever it is. We have got to be filled with God and His Spirit, not anything else. Why? Because we need to make the best use of our time (point 2). Life is short. Don't waste life in ways that will make you forget most of life.

5. Fill your mind with God-things. Verse 21 says our hearts should be filled with spiritual songs and God's truth. Man, we just need to get our minds out of the trash that the world offers us and put God-stuff in our minds. I have had some weekends in my life where I sat around binge-watching movies and TV. Fun stuff. Not a sin. BUT at the end of the weekend, I am feeling a little regret. I did not accomplish anything all weekend, nor did I become a better person. Besides that, there is just a bunch of crap in my head. It would be so much better to fill my mind with anything of God. Life is short. Get more God in you.

6. Look at verse 21. Submit to others. Wait a minute—submit? That means like giving in to other people and letting them have their way. No, I want my way. Well, actually submitting means caring for others so much that I do give some of my time to them. I do want to give them what they need to be better. I do want to show them God. Why does life always need to be about me? We need to be prepared to sacrifice some of our time for the good of others. Who has God put in your life? How can you show them God?

See, we do this "out of reverence for Christ." We do this because we honor God by honoring others. This world has too many people fighting for their own honor and not living to honor others. God wants us to be the ones to change that. Life is too short to waste. Be like Christ and think about others.

Remember, God's grace takes care of your past so you can hold your future in your hand. Is God with you? Are you letting Him control you? Make goals. Every day, fill your mind with God's stuff. That is always good use of your time.

Easter is the biggest holiday of the year for followers of Jesus. We should remember what Jesus did for us every day, but especially at this time of year. The Friday before Easter is known as Good Friday, where we remember Christ's death. Sunday is when we remember that He did not stay dead but rose again to conquer death and sin for us on Easter. Some of the best verses to read about what happened are **John chapters 18–21** and **Luke 22–24**, and I encourage you to read those chapters this weekend. But today, let's look at a famous chapter in the Old Testament that told what Jesus would do when he came to earth—**Isaiah 53**. Read that chapter now, and let's see a few thoughts from here.

1.   People did not appreciate Jesus.

Verse 3 really nails it. He was rejected and despised, just like today. Why? Is it because we don't like people that are better than us because their lives remind us of our faults and sins? Are we just jealous? Were people jealous of the attention Jesus was getting? At the end of the day, do we just care about ourselves and not others, so no one stood with Jesus because, well, "I've got to watch out for myself"? I think all of this is true. I think we can all find ourselves in that mess of thinking. So, in the end, Jesus was a "man of sorrows" who really knew "grief." He grieved for us; He was saddened by our sin and our rejection of His answer for our sin.

2.   He died a horrible death.

In verse 5, we see Jesus was "pierced" and "crushed" for us. Hanging on a cross with nails through your body was a brutal way to die. He had also been whipped and beaten. In **Isaiah 52:14**, it says that He was beaten so badly that His appearance did not even look human anymore. Yet (53:7), He did not complain or curse the people beating Him.

3.   He died for our sin.

It is clear that he went through all of this for our sin. Verse 5 tells us He was crushed for our sins. -Verse 6 reminds us that we are merely stupid sheep who keep turning off the right path and onto the path of sin—and yet it was for us on that path of sin that Jesus died. Verses 10–11 tell us that this was God's plan. It was God's way of showing us that He truly loves us. God did not merely tell us that He loves us; God showed us that He loves us through Jesus. And now, if we know Him, we can be "accounted righteous" in God's sight. That means that even though we are sinners, God will look at us and say that we are righteous because He sees that Jesus paid our debt for us. Jesus took care of our sin.

4.   He did not stay dead.

Easter day is a Sunday to remember that Jesus rose from the dead that day. Verse 12 refers to Jesus being exalted for eternity—that His inheritance is glorious (see **52:13** also). Again, this was God's plan—it was His way of showing us how much He loves us. God is holy and righteous while we are not. We are sinners who have chosen our own way. Jesus is the true way (**John 14:6**). Easter shows God's power over sin.

5.   God wants us.

All of this is because God really loves us and wants to have us come to Him. Like, He really wants us—He really wants you. Read **Isaiah 55:1–7**. These are amazing verses! God tells us, <u>pleads</u> with us to come to Him. He says why would we chase other things in this life that do not satisfy? Think about it—does money really satisfy? Does living for whatever else you have been living for really satisfy? Is this it? No, God is the end all, and He truly gives us reason for living, and He calls and wants the one who has no money (that is us)! God is offering His love to us for free because Jesus paid it all, and God loves us that much. But will you get closer to Him? He will not force you to accept Him. He knows what you and I have done and tells us to come anyway so He can show us "compassion." What beautiful verses! But you need to come to Him. He is calling us this Easter— calling us to come, be close to Him, and experience the compassion of God. Sadly, many of us will keep chasing the worthlessness of this world. We will not seek Him "while he may be found." Don't let that be you. May this Easter be a time of renewal between you and God. Tell Him how you feel, and accept His love and compassion for you. Chase Him above all else in this life.

About the Author

Chaplain Paul Beliasov was a teacher for two years in the United States before going to Bangladesh in 1992. He continued as a missionary and teacher in Bangladesh until 2011 and then in Indonesia from 2012 until 2019, when he returned full time to the United States and joined Good News Jail and Prison Ministry as a chaplain at York County Prison. Chaplain Paul loves getting to know God better, spending time outdoors with his family, reading, and playing basketball. He lives in Pennsylvania with his wife and three children.